The Apostasy of a High Priest

The Sociology of an American Cult

Park B. Romney

INFINITY
PUBLISHING

For more information see politac.org

ISBN 978-0-7414-6294-7

Printed in the United States of America

Published June 2011

INFINITY PUBLISHING
1094 New DeHaven Street, Suite 100
West Conshohocken, PA 19428-2713
Toll-free (877) BUY BOOK
Local Phone (610) 941-9999
Fax (610) 941-9959
Info@buybooksontheweb.com
www.buybooksontheweb.com

Those who say religion has nothing to do with politics
do not know what religion is

Mahatma Gandhi
1869-1948

To my grandchildren
who will likely never know me for who I am,
May you find happiness, peace, and security in truth.

———————————

To investigators
of The Church of Jesus Christ of Latter Day Saints,
I hope you will find these thoughts helpful in your quest.

———————————

To those who joined
the LDS Church as a result of my efforts,
Please forgive me.

———————————

To those persecuted, isolated, or abandoned for dissent,
You are not alone.

To the friends of Hugh,

Thank you.

Contents

Chapter 1

Obliged to Speak Out

My name is Park B. Romney. I am a former High Priest of the Church of Jesus Christ of Latter Day Saints, more commonly called the Mormon Church. On December 14, 2004, I asked, by formal letter, to have my name removed from the records of the Mormon Church for philosophical reasons. Simply put, I no longer believed in the Mormon Church's divine authority. I was advised in writing that my request was granted and that I was no longer a member of the Mormon Church on March 15, 2005. The purpose of this book is to share the philosophical journey that led me to the conclusion that I could no longer support the claim of divinity of the Mormon Church, and to acknowledge with forthright candor that the course of my life has impacted on the lives of others to whom I owe an explanation.

As a young man, like so many other young Mormon men and women, I served a proselytizing mission for the Church. For two years, in South America, I dedicated myself to seeking out and teaching prospective members of the Church. The objective was converting and baptizing people into Church membership. I was involved in the conversion of a number of people during this mission and after. Some of those converts, in turn, served missions themselves, bringing more converts to the Church. Many had children who they raised in the Mormon faith. I did my best to raise my children in the Mormon faith as long as I believed it. I can't name all of those I taught through the years. I do, however, believe that I have some responsibility to explain myself for the benefit of those whose lives may have been impacted by my "testimony" of the truthfulness of the Church.

In each and every case, where I was involved with the conversion of another to the Mormon Church, I shared my "testimony" with the individual as part of that process. In its more complete and proper form, a "testimony" of the truthfulness of the Church, for a Mormon, would include the declaration of one's own personal conviction that God lives; that Jesus Christ is the Son of God and Divine Mediator through whom salvation and exaltation (defined later) is made possible for all souls; that the *Book of Mormon* is true; that the late prophet, Joseph Smith, was, in fact, a true prophet, seer, and revelator of God, through whom essential priesthood "keys" of authority to act in the name of God were restored to the earth; that the current president of the Mormon Church is a true prophet, seer, and revelator of God; and that the Mormon Church, itself, is uniquely endowed with the only true priesthood authority of Jesus Christ to officiate in the administration of "saving ordinances" that are required for the eternal progress and exaltation of all souls.

These are not small claims. They should not be taken lightly. They have very significant meaning and ramifications. A conviction of these essential core beliefs, combined with specific compliance with the Mormon teachings on the subjects of chastity and fidelity; a certain health code involving, at a minimum, abstinence from the consumption of alcoholic beverages, tobacco, or recreational drugs; honesty and fair dealing with one's fellow man; and the ongoing payment of honest tithes to the Church, amounting to a full ten percent of one's annual income, at a minimum, are required of each member for "temple worthiness". This "temple worthiness" entitles the qualifying member of the Church to a "temple recommend" signed by priesthood officials of the Church on the basis of a determination of such worthiness. This "temple recommend" is presented to sentries at the entrance of Mormon temples and is required for entry into the temple. Without a current "temple recommend", not even a member of the Mormon Church can enter a Mormon temple. Weekly congregational meetings, for Mormons, are not held in the Mormon temples, but in chapels designated for that purpose. These meetings are open to all members of the Mormon Church and the public. The point of these meetings is to encourage "eternal progress", beginning with baptism, and culminating in temple ordinances including the ordinance of "temple marriage". Generally speaking, "civil marriages", or marriages outside the Mormon temples, are seen as a disappointing indication of a lack of worthiness to active members of the Mormon Church.

It is a specific matter of Mormon doctrine that a marriage performed in a Mormon temple by a uniquely authorized Mormon priesthood officiator is absolutely required for exaltation in the Kingdom of God, in the hereafter, or life after death. Exaltation is believed by Mormons to be a God-like state of existence also referred to as "Celestial Life". You don't qualify for exaltation in the Kingdom of God, in the next life, or even to witness your own daughter or son's temple marriage in this life, unless you are "worthy" by certain minimum Mormon standards, including making consistent contributions of ten percent of all of your income to the Church. With membership now reported to be well above twelve million members world-wide, and with a full-time missionary force reported to be in excess of fifty thousand, it is no small wonder that the Mormon Church is one of the wealthiest privately controlled organizations on the planet and rapidly becoming one of the most politically significant. Mormons, arguably as much as any other religious group, and more than most, are generally obedient to the teachings and declarations of their prophet and his local priesthood representatives. A Mormon Bishop, who is the congregational priesthood leader at the most local organized levels of the Church, wields enormous influence with his congregation. A Mormon Bishopric, generally, consists of three ordained High Priests of the local Mormon congregation, one of whom is called to serve as the Bishop, with the other two as his Counselors. I served as a Counselor in two successive Mormon Bishoprics. I asked to be released from my "calling" as Counselor, having become troubled over things I witnessed as a part of my experiences in my Church service. This began my own introspective philosophical inquiry into my beliefs and the doctrines of the Church. This inquiry ultimately led me to feel morally compelled to request that my name be removed from the records of the Church. I could not continue, in good faith, to support the claims of the Church about its own unique and divine authority to minister and officiate on behalf of God on earth.

I would very much like all those with whom I shared my testimony about the truthfulness of the Church in the past to know that I did so with the utmost sincerity at the time, believing, with all of my heart, that it was true. Upon realizing that I had countenanced things that left me with serious questions about the truthfulness of the claims of the Church, I never again testified as to the truthfulness of the Church, and I ceased to participate in any ordinances for which the use of my priesthood would be a requirement. I ceased partaking of the weekly sacrament prepared by the priesthood members authorized to do so, and ceased attending the Mormon temple even though my "temple worthiness recommend" had not expired. I made these adjustments of my own free will and choice long before anyone, with the exception of a couple of very close friends, knew why I was making them. When my eldest daughter was married in the temple I chose to wait outside the temple with a current temple recommend in my possession at the time, because, on the basis of my own knowledge of my own unworthiness by the standards discussed above, I did not want to be a hypocrite, or in any way dishonest about what I knew and believed. I had not yet shared the significant shifts in my philosophical beliefs. Needless to say, this was a great disappointment to my family and somewhat dismaying to some. No one really understood the deeply sincere philosophical shift in my beliefs. It was easy to assume that I was simply a sinner who hadn't paid his tithing or was guilty of some other moral infraction. The extent of my apostasy was not known or understood. In my case, I had not only come to believe that the Church was false, but also, on the basis of that belief, entered into behavior that would have been seen as sin by the Church even though it was not known at the time.

The concept, or notion, that a High Priest of the Mormon Church might, out of strength rather than weakness, choose to abstain from the outward ordinances and practices of the Church on the basis of his own moral and philosophical courage, because he had thoughtfully and sincerely reconsidered what he ultimately would find himself compelled to acknowledge to be false, does not exist in the Mormon theology. The unique view of "apostasy" from the Mormon Church was taught by the founding Mormon prophet, Joseph Smith, and others, to frequently involve a false quest for moral superiority by the apostate. According to Mormon theology, the notion that a former Mormon might profess to seek a higher moral or philosophical plane by leaving the Church is conclusive evidence of Satan's power over them. Among other things, Joseph Smith is reported to have taught, "That man who rises up to condemn others, finding fault with the Church, saying that they are out of the way, *while he himself is righteous*, then know assuredly, that that man is in the high road to apostasy..." (Joseph Smith, Jr., 1805-1844. Compare to *Teachings of the Prophet Joseph Smith*, p. 156.) Joseph Smith is also reported to have said, "Strange as it may appear at first thought, yet it is no less strange than true, that notwithstanding all the professed determination to live godly, apostates after turning from the faith of Christ, unless they have speedily repented, have sooner or later fallen into the snares of the wicked one, and have been left destitute of the Spirit of God, to manifest their wickedness in the eyes of multitudes." (Joseph Smith, Jr., 1805-1844. Compare to *Teachings of the Prophet Joseph Smith*, p. 67.) As it turns out, according to the Mormon view, leaving the Mormon Church constitutes "turning from the faith of Christ" since they view themselves as Christ's exclusive agents.

Needless to say, this circular view of apostasy contributes to a great deal of strain in the family relationships of someone who decides to leave the Mormon Church on moral or philosophical grounds. An acknowledged sinner, amongst Mormons, is likely to experience an increase in the love that manifests itself in the actual fellowship from their Mormon family and friends as they attempt to reclaim the sinner. Such a person is seen as potentially humble and teachable. Such are socially and spiritually worth the continued investment.

An apostate, on the other hand, who makes a choice to leave the Church on the basis of skepticism or disbelief in the authenticity of the Church's claim of unique, divine authority from God, or disappointment with other doctrines of the Church, and who sees himself as pursuing a philosophical approach to life that requires of him a more rigid standard of ethics and system of validating the truths he will choose to live by than the Church teaches, is invariably condemned as a prideful and arrogant follower of Satan. Such an individual is now disqualified for full participation in discussion with his former Mormon family and friends in matters of theology, religion, ethics, general morality, and certainly not Mormon behavior, doctrine, or history. A Mormon apostate becomes a pariah among most Mormons, whose presence is tolerated only to the extent that the apostate is willing to keep his mouth shut in matters of religious philosophy or subjects that might be threatening to their faith.

Needless to say, apostasy from the Mormon Church is a very difficult social choice, with enormous ramifications, for someone from a prominent and devout Mormon family. The pain and heartache of certain forms of being somewhat socially, intellectually, and philosophically ostracized are inevitable. Such pains are beyond the scope of this book. The purpose of this book is to explain the philosophical journey that led to my abandonment of the faith of my family and the corresponding decision to leave the Mormon Church.

Chapter 2

The Substance of Faith

Each of us is born into this world in a state of complete dependency on someone else who loves us enough to help us survive and develop. Complete dependency is the beginning of the human condition. Whether by the intelligent design of a divine Creator or the natural selective process of millions of years of elimination, the human infant is born into this world in a complete state of dependency. This reality is integral to who and what we are. Our species cannot survive without the nurturing and caring of our infants. As infants, newly born into this world, we are relatively undeveloped, emotionally and intellectually. Certainly we will have genetic propensities. We may also have unique physical or intellectual limitations or strengths associated with our development experience in the womb. It still remains true, however, that within the confines of our genetic propensities and other strengths or weaknesses associated with our development as embryos, we emerge into this world with a relatively clean emotional and intellectual slate, ready for the life programming that begins at that point.

The relationship that follows birth, between an infant and the primary caregiver, is one in which a form of crude communication is established. A newborn infant communicates through the initial "binary code" of crying. There are two fundamental components in this coded communication. "Sound on", and "sound off" make up the initial code. Quickly thereafter, an increasing pattern of responses to the code formulates the basis of understanding upon which variations of the code emerge. "Sound loud". "Sound soft". "Sound loud, with a grimace" or "sound low, with a cue or a sigh". This increasingly sophisticated code is developed largely on the basis of the shared experience between the infant and the caregiver. The responsiveness to the variations of the code is processed by the infant's brain. Adjustments in the patterns of code are stimulated as a result of the brain's processed evaluation of the caregiver's responsive inputs or actions. The iterations of these interactions and adjustments give rise to the increasingly complex form of communication between the two. This becomes the growing basis of understanding that develops between them and through which the infant's limited grasp of the realities of the world expands. As this coded form of communication develops and is used consistently, an amazing development quickly emerges between the infant and the caregiver. This development is anticipation. Almost as soon as the infant connects patterns of sounds with the stimulus that is most commonly found to be associated with them, anticipation of that stimulus begins to result from those sounds. Caregivers quickly recognize the emergence of the phenomena of anticipation. On the basis of this recognition, caregivers begin, intentionally, to make sounds that the infant will recognize in order to soothe the infant with anticipation of the stimulus demanded. This subtle adjustment in the interactive relationship between the caregiver and the infant begins the experiential basis of consistency and credibility between them. If the caregiver treats the emerging understanding of the infant's anticipations, associated with certain sounds, with respect and consistency by validating the anticipation with the stimulus that the sound suggested would follow, a subconscious form of trust emerges between the two. This trust manifests itself in a comfort level that becomes apparent in the behavior of the infant. Increasingly, the infant trusts in the presence of the familiar caregiver. This trust increases the level of anticipation that the infant associates with the input from the caregiver. Through this process the initial development of the roots of faith begins at the subconscious level, even in an infant.

Faith emerges upon the convergence of an experientially based sense of anticipation with a subconscious awareness of what actions or other stimuli are likely to give rise to related responsive events. When the convergence of anticipation with related awareness of relevant connections between stimuli and resulting or responsive events gives rise to an actual investment of energy, for the express purpose of bringing to pass such an event, an act of faith has occurred. Faith is clearly beyond belief. It involves actions in anticipation of results. Faith is a human manifestation of confidence. Faith brings about an investment of targeted energy with a desired result in mind. These early manifestations of faith do not require processing at the conscious level. They are simply programmed responses to survival related interactions that are triggered at the brain chemistry level. They result in consistent patterns of synaptic firings in the brain that contribute to the creation of memory traces. These synaptic firings and memory traces are consistently validated, or reinforced, by the human brain and body's own survival instincts as feelings of comfort or discomfort arise. In this way the feelings of trust that an infant develops in the caregiver occur at the biological and physiological level, beneath the level of consciousness. Feelings of comfort are understandably imprinted in the infant's memory with the sounds, and smells, and feelings associated with the caregiver's very presence. If the caregiver respects this process, and employs what I will call "integrity" in the management of this relationship, an increasing measure of trust can be developed between the caregiver and the infant, transferring into childhood. This integrity would amount to the avoidance of confusion in the infant with stimuli that is inconsistent with normally associated events. The resulting trusting process that comes out of this relationship precedes the more advanced development of the infant's intellectual processing at the conscious level. As the level of verbalized communication between the child and caregiver becomes more sophisticated over time, the trust phenomenon is increasingly complimented with verbal statements. Increasingly, verbal statements are processed at the conscious level while other stimuli, associated with the feelings of anticipation that are validated by satisfying events, are still processed at the subconscious level. In this way, a child comes to "feel" a sense of truth associated with a caregiver's statements before the infant develops the intellectual capacity to evaluate the philosophical truth of statements at the conscious level. As such, it is not only easy but almost unavoidable that children become programmed to believe what mom says. This programming becomes such a tightly conditioned response in children to their mothers that they will, more often than not, continue to experience the feeling of trust while skipping the intellectual process of consciously evaluating the statements of mother, even when they have the intellectual capacity to do so. Because this phenomena is so real, and so consistently a part of the development of a child, it is understandable that the process of objectively evaluating statements for their philosophical truth is something that has to be taught. It doesn't come entirely naturally. To the contrary, the process of conscious intellectual evaluation has to be introduced to the brain with considerable encouragement after years of subconscious habit patterns that have a tendency to undermine it. The warm and "fuzzy" feelings associated with skipping this process, and simply accepting what mom said to be true just because she said so, come more naturally.

Most of us are physiologically programmed to feel trust in what mom says. Most moms don't care to teach objectivity. Not very many moms in the world will resist the ever present temptation that the power they have over the minds and hearts of their children gives rise to. Most all moms will take advantage of the enormous power of programmed credibility that they have developed with their children to indoctrinate them to believe what they want them to believe to be true while encouraging the child to skip the intellectual process of objective evaluation. This situation is further complicated, or, depending on the perspective, simplified, when moms reward their children with artificial incentives for demonstrating a belief in what the mom wishes them to believe. These incentives can sometimes be tangible gifts, such as candy or some other treat, or intangible rewards, such as smiles of approval, accolades, or hugs. Children develop powerful subconscious attachments to the approval of their trusted caregivers. As children move from childhood into adolescence, they are increasingly thrust into a challenging world while the reassurance of their trusted caregivers is weaned away by the simple complications of life. They see mom less, and they see the kids at school, who tend to poke fun at anything, more. Consequently, the disorienting feeling of growing up leaves adolescents wanting for the warm and fuzzy feeling of reassurance previously associated with mom. They seek the feelings of security and reassurance wherever they may be found. Often, this will be reflected in their choice of friends, which is primarily driven by who accepts them warmly and readily into a clique offering social support amidst the increasing turmoil that school actually is for adolescents. Acceptance is a key. Adolescents, very often, are only too willing to exchange one set of beliefs for another, simply to maintain the social alliances that require the change. They will easily convince themselves that their adjustments have been well thought through, finding superficial faults with their previous beliefs if necessary, and finding equally superficial validation for the new beliefs. Their mothers, after all, did not teach them the rigors or importance of critical thinking and objective analysis. Most moms want their kids to believe what they want them to believe, and do not see teaching their kids to thoroughly question what they want them to believe to be a very good way to achieve that end. And so it is that

adolescents, and most adults who never mature philosophically far beyond the adolescent stage, may change their
beliefs from time to time, but rarely make significant
adjustments to the process of validation by which they arrive
at those beliefs. What changes, more often than not, is the
support group whose approval is the object, not the process
of epistemology, or reasoning, by which their belief system
is validated.

So, what becomes of faith? What might have become a
profoundly reassuring and increasing sense of driving
confidence, due to consistent validation of actions driven by
anticipation of desirable results amidst an increasing
intellectual capacity to evaluate truth and reality, often
degenerates into a vague and increasingly fragmented system
of contrived justification. The disparity between what is
anticipated and what actually follows an investment in the
actions that are supposed to bring about the desired results
breaks down what might have been a growing confidence. I
contend, contrary to many atheists, that faith was never the
problem. The object of faith, and the understanding of what
faith actually is, is the problem.

I was taught, in my childhood, to believe that the Church of
Jesus Christ of Latter Day Saints, which we referred to as the
Mormon Church, was true. I was taught to believe that all of
the warm and "fuzzy" feelings that I associated with the
goodness of mother, and hearth, and home, emanated from
the Holy Ghost, who, by those feelings, was manifesting to
me that the Church of Jesus Christ of Latter Day Saints was
true. I believed what I was taught. My mother told me so.
Over time, I studied the scriptures, including the *Book of
Mormon*. I acquired the "testimony" that was promised, in
the form of a warm and glowing feeling in my heart that the
Church was true. My mother told me I would. I tried hard, as
a young man, to be a good person. My mother told me I
should. When I was a good person, I felt good about myself.

My mother told me I would, and others reinforced that when I was. This warmed my heart. I was consistently told that those feelings in my heart were from The Holy Ghost, confirming to me that the Mormon Church was true. I believed what I was told. I got lots of hugs and validation for believing what I was told, so I became more vocal about what I believed. When I became more vocal, I got even more hugs and validation. I was a good boy. I felt good a lot. Surely, I thought, the Mormon Church must, therefore, be true. I had faith that it was. I came to believe that if I followed the teachings of the Mormon Church good stuff would happen to me, either in this life, or the life to come, or both. I really wanted good stuff to happen to me. So I tried really hard to follow the teachings of the Mormon Church. Mostly, the good stuff that happened to me was that I got lots of approval and accolades from my Mormon family and friends for the depth of my convictions and the extent of my self-sacrificing Church service. That got me by for a long time. I had lots of faith, I thought, because I kept doing what the Church taught that I should do, to the best of my ability, even when bad things happened. I was told that bad stuff happening was a test of my faith, and if I passed that test even better things would happen. "Passing the test" was understood to be enduring misfortune with faith. That seemed reasonable. I had faith, and I was surrounded by lots of Mormon friends and family members who thought I was a really good person, and they treated me very well. My family was a very prominent Mormon family with many examples of considerable successes in the world among my relatives. Clearly, I thought, good stuff happened to faithful Mormons. I wanted good stuff to happen to me, too. I believed it would, either in this life, or the life to come. Preferably, both.

Chapter 3

The Validation of Truth

After some time in my life, I came to wonder about my faith. I just wasn't all that thrilled with the good stuff happening in my life. I was still getting accolades for my devotion to the Church, but my work wasn't going all that well. I was increasingly becoming a more thoughtful guy. I thought that being more thoughtful was a good thing. Unfortunately, as it turns out, a lot of people don't think thoughtful is a particularly good thing. I probably vocalized too much of what I thought. The more thoughtful I became, it seemed, the fewer accolades I was getting about my devotion to the Church. I thought about the blessings that I kept hearing about in the lives of faithful members of the Church. It seemed that many members of the Church experienced blessings like financial stability. Financial stability would have been a very nice blessing to have. I paid my tithing to the Church, faithfully. Financial stability was often promised as a blessing associated with paying tithing faithfully. It seemed my "career", for lack of a better term, was not reflecting my devotion to being a faithful tithe payer. I continued to experience what seemed like a very odd pattern of bad luck in my work. In a two year period I was trying to make a "go" of being a mortgage loan representative. I had family members and friends who were doing quite well in that business, and they encouraged me to give it a try. Everyone seemed to think I was doing all the right things. My clients seemed to like my work and refer me to their friends. Unfortunately, four separate loan companies folded up consecutively, right out from under me, forcing me to go find another job each time. It seemed I had that kind of luck. It became troubling to me that my bad luck seemed to have a larger impact on my career than my devotion to being a full tithe payer.

Other things made me thoughtful. I served in a couple of Mormon Bishoprics, as a Counselor, and was increasingly becoming dismayed at things I observed in connection with that service. In fairness to the Bishops with whom I served, I should point out that it was not their particular conduct that gave rise to my questions. It had more to do with other things, peripheral to their immediate jurisdictions, but within my observable vantage point as a Counselor in those Bishoprics. Mormons believe that a man who serves in responsible positions of priesthood authority is "called of God" and endowed with the powers of "revelation" necessary to serve effectively in his "calling". I won't belabor a full discussion of everything I observed while serving as a Counselor in two consecutive Bishoprics that gave rise to my questions about these powers of revelation associated with callings. That would be beyond the scope of this book and un-necessary. Suffice it to say, for the moment, that I began to wonder about how reliable the inspiration of the priesthood actually was. It was beginning to seem rather "hit and miss" to me. I couldn't help but observe, on a number of occasions, that the insight that I would have thought to be commonly found among beer swilling sophomores at a frat party exceeded some of the inspiration I saw attributed to God by Mormon priesthood authorities. Not always, just occasionally. Unfortunately, some of those occasions had very significant negative impacts on people's lives. I became quite thoughtful about that.

Mormon priesthood leaders, generally, were relatively good, well intentioned people, in my observation. Many, if not most of their priesthood decisions, seemed quite supportable. However, there were just too many things, for my comfort level, that I just had a real hard time with. It was difficult, for instance, to reconcile the notion of an all knowing God, who was just and fair, actively leading His Church through his priesthood representatives where injustices or inequities seemed too common. It seemed more, to me, like well meaning fallible men were struggling to navigate through their own biases, political pressure, and personal agendas, to find their way, sometimes, to decisions that they would then attribute to God and inspiration in order to get support from people who might have had a hard time supporting the same decision otherwise. Not all the time. Enough times for me to become thoughtful about the reliability of the Church's claim to divine authority from God. I began to wonder about things like statistics and probability. Simple things, like, "What percentage of time does one of my loan processors need to be obviously wrong about something before I begin to question the reliability of their judgment or credibility altogether?" Would that be a big number, like ninety percent? Or, would it be a smaller number, like thirty percent? If three out of ten times, when I told clients that their loan was approved, it actually turned out to be just wrong, how long could I continue to expect loan referrals from real estate offices? Should priesthood decisions or edicts attributed to God be held to the same standard of credibility as business representations? Or should there be some more lenient standard in matters involving the professed authority of God? People, including myself, were coming to priesthood leaders for guidance in decisions that would have a major impact that they or others would sometimes have to live with for the rest of their lives. I became thoughtful about such things.

It really wouldn't bother me so much if I went to a friend for advice and he told me his point of view, which clearly reflected a certain bias or personal agenda, and then added, "…but that's just me, you need to make your own decision". It wouldn't bother me if a Bishop said the same thing. Where it becomes a different matter is when certain "counsel" is presented under the "color of God's authority", and your worthiness in God's kingdom is tied to your willingness to follow the "counsel". Let's say your worthiness to be in attendance at your daughter's wedding is part of the equation. See what I mean? Would it seem reasonable to you that the standards applied in considering the credibility of the claim of inspiration would have to be fairly high before submitting yourself in obedience to an authorized representative of God under such circumstances? Or, had you already come to that conclusion on the basis of the notion of giving up a full ten percent of your annual income? For me, it wasn't the temple attendance thing or the tithing thing that got me thinking about the credibility of the Church's claim of divine authority and revelation. It's funny what triggers the sensibilities of different people. For me, it was simple matters of injustice imposed on members other than myself. Things that just weren't fair. Often these things were simple, but clear.

In one "ward" (a congregation) of the Church, an elderly divorced woman was struggling to make ends meet. Her husband, who lived in another "ward" of the Church in a different state, hadn't been paying alimony under the terms of their court ordered settlement agreement for a number of years. She found it somewhat offensive that her ex-husband, who was a member of a very prominent and politically significant Mormon family, still enjoyed the use of a "temple worthiness recommend", since it is a matter of Church policy that "temple worthiness recommends" are not issued to members who are in default in their alimony or child support payments. On numerous occasions she sent letters to both her own priesthood leaders and his priesthood leaders raising the obvious questions. In those letters she consistently offered conclusive proof from court records that he had an alimony obligation and that he was in default in paying it. I have seen the documentary evidence. It is unquestionable. I have also seen written acknowledgement of the receipt of her correspondence from the priesthood leaders, including this evidence. This man, amidst this controversy, was called by the Church authorities to serve three consecutive full time missions, for two years each, in which he would devote full time efforts on behalf of the Church, without pay, to further the missionary work of the Church. The objective of the Church's missionary efforts is, obviously, the recruitment of converts by baptism into the Church. Worthiness for baptism into the Church includes a promise to pay an honest tithe to the Church. So this man, at the behest of the Church, would spend six years of labor, for free, contributing to increases in the Church's revenues at the expense of his ex-wife's financial stability. All told, his alimony arrearage grew to over eighty three thousand dollars during this missionary service. Each of these missionary calls would have to have been endorsed by his Bishop; then his Stake President, who was a regional priesthood authority; then a General Authority of the Church, who was another High Priest with specific charge of Church mission calls; and finally, by the President of the Church, who is sustained as a prophet, seer, and revelator. Each subordinate priesthood official is believed to be endowed by specific delegation of priesthood authority with all of the "keys, rights, and powers of revelation pertinent to their calling". So, God's representatives were "all over" each of these three callings, at every level of review, with all of the required power and insight of Godliness to vet out any potential problems. Still, amidst conclusive evidence of the default, this man was called to serve three consecutive two-year missions while his ex-wife got "stiffed". Here, not just one priesthood leader had an "off day", which would have been quite understandable. The entire chain of command appears to have repeatedly misfired in amazing lockstep unison, amidst repeated offerings of conclusive documentary evidence of the problem, receipt of which having been acknowledged in writing. The man was, after all, a member of a very prominent and politically significant Mormon family. Conversely, had this gentleman consulted with a beer swilling sophomore at a frat party about his missionary callings under the circumstances, I think he might have been told, "Gee, dude, instead of working for the Church for free, I mean as long as you're willing and able to work, dude, why not get a real job and pay your alimony?"

Now this was not the only situation where I observed what seemed to be patently obvious examples of injustice perpetrated under "color of priesthood authority". However, it is, perhaps, among the most clearly useful in pointing out with clarity the underlying philosophical questions that apply. These are men who profess to represent God, Himself, in their insistence that your worthiness for His kingdom depends, in significant part, on your contribution of ten percent of your income to their coffers. It would appear that the recruitment of contributing tithe payers turns out to be quite a high relative priority to the God that they represent, even higher, say, than the temple worthiness standard of honesty and fair dealing with one's fellow man or ex-wife. Of course, there will be those who argue that this isolated situation is just an example of the fallibility of humans, and not a sound or sufficient basis to cast aspersions on the "still valid" claims of divine authority of this priesthood. I think this "isolated boo-boo defense" of the Mormon priesthood is a reasonable argument that might fairly be considered in evaluating the claims of the priesthood, but not so compelling an argument that the woman, or anyone else aware of the situation, should be branded as an unforgiving complainer for having fundamental questions about the responsibilities of the Church, and its role in this matter, and the relevance of this situation to the evaluation of their claims of divine authority and revelation. In short, I think the obvious questions that arise are valid questions, not malicious questions. The woman will suffer the financial instability occasioned by this situation for the rest of her life.

Her husband has now transferred all of his assets out of his own name, rendering her court judgment against him for the unpaid alimony uncollectible. He is now no longer able to work at all, for health reasons. She is now over 80 years old. Her children's lives will be affected as her care will increasingly fall to their responsibility where they are financially able to assist. The Church is currently subsidizing her rent from funds made available to assist the "needy". She wouldn't be "needy" if the Church had counseled her ex-husband to get a job for those six years and apply proceeds to the payment of her alimony during that time, instead of availing itself of his free labor. Nor would she be needy if the Church had paid for the labor of the missionary work on the condition that the money was to be applied to her alimony. When her children contribute from time to time to her financial needs she is expected to apply those contributions to her rent, thereby reducing the Church's welfare subsidy. I am considered to be an unforgiving heathen by many Mormons for suggesting that there is something morally wrong with this situation. According to Church theology, as it applies to apostasy, the notion that there is a higher morality than what is demonstrated in this scenario, and that I should aspire to that higher morality outside the Church, while criticizing the Church over this, is conclusive evidence of my alliance with Satan.

In fairness, let's consider, for conversation sake, that the man may have cheated on his taxes for a number of years and now found he was under the burden of a federal tax lien that exceeded the amount of his alimony arrearage. Any assets or income under such a scenario would be subject to seizure by the Internal Revenue Service. By transferring his assets into the names of others, he might be able to protect his assets from seizure and avoid the loss of his home. Since any income would be subject to seizure he might as well dedicate his time for free to the Church, because he isn't going to see any of it anyway. His unpaid alimony would be the least of his problems. Still, is this a scenario in which a man would be considered worthy of a "temple worthiness recommend" by the standards of a just God who denies temple attendance to others for alimony arrearage? Would it be appropriate for this man to be sent on a mission to call upon others to repent of their sins and come to the waters of baptism? How would a just God choose to be represented? Are these not fair questions?

Situations like this leave me thoughtful. They have, over the years, given rise to questions, in my mind, about the appropriate methodology for the validation of truth. Mormon "fast and testimony meetings" are held monthly. The meetings are "kicked off" by a member of the local priesthood leadership sharing his testimony of the truthfulness of the Church with the congregation. The time is then turned over to the congregation so that members, on an impromptu basis, can share their own testimonies of the truthfulness of the Church. "I know that the Church is true", is the common declaration, or, more formally, "I testify that the Church is true". Typically the member will share some heartwarming experience that they see as a recent reaffirmation for them that the "Church is true". What does that mean, "The Church is true"?

I would venture to guess, on the basis of my experience in the Church, that the majority of Church members who share their testimonies in these monthly meetings are motivated to do so as a result of some recent event in their lives that gave rise to heartwarming feelings. Mormons are taught from a very early age, if they are raised in the Church, to recognize heartwarming feelings to be manifestations of the Holy Ghost, confirming to them the truthfulness of the Church. Consequently, feelings of comfort, security, consolation, compassion, and many other such comfort moments often give rise to a belief in Mormons that they have, yet again, experienced a witness from the Holy Ghost as to the truthfulness of the Church in general, or the truthfulness of a specific teaching, or principle, that is being presented when the feelings arise, or a specific answer to a prayer that precipitated the feelings. It's all about that warm feeling in the heart. Devout Mormons seek to <u>feel</u> truth. This is how they are taught to recognize truth. It is not about objective evaluation. It is about "spiritual manifestations" of heartwarming feelings. There are very significant doctrinal reasons for this in the Mormon theology. There are also very practical reasons for this, as they relate to the simple dynamics of the conversion process. The Church capitalizes on the realities that relate to the very emergence of faith in an infant, and the programmed synaptic sequences that remain largely in place in all humans and that cause them to feel comfortable, under certain circumstances, while skipping the process of intellectual evaluation and adopting a "truth" on the basis of certain feelings.

A certain branch of philosophy, called epistemology, deals with the theory of knowledge and its corollary questions including, "What is knowledge?", and, "How do we know what we know?" To an engineer, involved in an effort to land a man on the moon, these questions have a great deal of significance. Recognizing the difference between what is known to be true and what is believed to be true is crucial. To an accused witch in the Salem witch trials of 1692, there would have been no more significant questions on earth. To Edwin Ovasapyan, falsely accused of murder in Glendale, California, in 2009, these questions must have been haunting as he spent 8 months in County Jail before he was exonerated from the charges. Apparently negligence and malice in dealing with exculpatory evidence cost the city of Glendale over one million dollars in damages awarded to this modern day victim of epistemological abuse.

I don't think the annals of religious history reflect a great deal of diligence, by any Church, to questions of epistemology. Amazingly, the *Book of Mormon* takes the subject matter on directly. Fundamental to the belief that the Mormon Church is true, is the belief that the *Book of Mormon* is true. So fundamental, in fact, that it has always been seen as a key cornerstone of the Mormon religion. Of course, the Mormon Church's continued viability and strength as an organized religion, and as one of the wealthiest international conglomerates in the world, is not derived from the unified belief in Jesus Christ. It is derived from the belief that the Mormon Church is the sole authorized agency on earth, exclusively endowed with the only true authority to act in the name of Jesus Christ and administer the ordinances that are absolutely required for exaltation in God's Kingdom. Acceptance of the *Book of Mormon* as a true and authentic ancient prophetic record is a key for three fundamental reasons, as follows: 1) The *Book of Mormon* bears witness to the divinity of Jesus Christ; 2) The *Book of Mormon* foretells of the restoration of the priesthood of Jesus Christ in these "Latter Days", through a prophet name Joseph; 3) The *Book of Mormon* sets forth the prescribed epistemology of the Church, which is vital to the conversion of its proselytes to a belief in the *Book of Mormon* itself, and, thereby, the Church's claims to authority in the ministry.

I would like to suggest that there are two fundamental approaches to the questions of epistemology that are differentiated by the relative value placed on two competing systems of validation, or differentiation, between knowledge and belief. I wouldn't be surprised if some professor of philosophy, somewhere, might disagree and call this an oversimplification of the subject matter. Of course, he would be right. It is useful, however, to illustrate a certain point. On one hand, there are those who would advocate that "knowledge" is best ascertained and differentiated from a hypothesis by suspending the reasoning process and turning to the heart for the feeling of truth. On the other hand, there are those who would advocate that knowledge is best ascertained by employing reasoning that is consistent with experimental validation and the gathering and analysis of factual evidence. Various hybrids of these two approaches to epistemology are generally seen in practice. However, make no mistake, whenever a hybrid form of the two is employed, the candidate will ultimately reveal his or her bias by the relative priority that is given to either the feeling of the heart or the objective analysis of relevant facts as they may be synoptically integrated into a system of harmonious knowledge in the absence of contradiction. Epistemology may, on the one hand, lead to a rigorous intellectual discipline, or, on the other hand, a subjective and potentially circular emotional whim.

The epistemology advocated in the *Book of Mormon* is an appeal to a circular form of self-convincing, beginning with and dependant on an unleashed desire for the outcome of conviction. While some might profess that it respects a form of objectivity in advocating "an experiment", the experiment advocated is thereafter revealed to be a form of fixation on the desire to believe, even to the point of openly discrediting skepticism, or the resistance of belief, on the basis of the, yet unfounded, suggestion that such skepticism would presumptively constitute resisting "the Spirit of the Lord". This remarkable speech is found in the teachings attributed to a prophet named Alma, as follows:

> Now, as I said concerning faith—that it was not a perfect knowledge—even so it is with my words. Ye cannot know of their surety at first, unto perfection, any more than faith is a perfect knowledge.

> But behold, if ye will awake and arouse your faculties, even to an experiment upon my words, and exercise a particle of faith, yea, even if ye can no more than desire to believe, let this desire work in you, even until ye believe in a manner that ye can give place for a portion of my words.

Now, we will compare the word unto a seed. Now, if ye give place, that a seed may be planted in your heart, behold, if it be a true seed, or a good seed, if ye do not cast it out by your unbelief, that ye will resist the Spirit of the Lord, behold, it will begin to swell within your breasts; and when you feel these swelling motions, ye will begin to say within yourselves—It must needs be that this is a good seed, or that the word is good, for it beginneth to enlarge my soul; yea, it beginneth too enlighten my understanding, yea, it beginneth to be delicious to me.

Now behold, would not this increase your faith? I say unto you, Yea; nevertheless it hath not grown up to a perfect knowledge.

But behold, as the seed swelleth, and sprouteth, and beginneth to grow, then you must needs say that the seed is good; for behold it swelleth, and sprouteth, and beginneth to grow. And now, behold, will not this strengthen your faith? Yea, it will strengthen your faith: for ye will say I know that this is a good seed; for behold it sprouteth and beginneth to grow.

And now, behold, are ye sure that this is a good seed? I say unto you, Yea; for every seed bringeth forth unto its own likeness.

Therefore, if a seed groweth it is good, but if it groweth not, behold it is not good, therefore it is cast away.

And now, behold, because ye have tried the experiment, and planted the seed, and it swelleth and sprouteth, and beginneth to grow, ye must needs know that the seed is good.

And now, behold, is your knowledge perfect? Yea, your knowledge is perfect in that thing, and your faith is dormant; and this because you know, for ye know that the word hath swelled your souls, and ye also know that it hath sprouted up, that your understanding doth begin to be enlightened, and your mind doth begin to expand. (*Book of Mormon, The Book of Alma.* Compare to pages 289-290 of the 1981 edition.)

In effect, Alma advocates that a conviction of the truth of his words can be achieved by fixating on a desire to believe his words are true until this desire fills the heart with a swelling feeling, deemed to be confirmation of the truth of his words. I'm sure Alma is correct. A conviction of just about anything can certainly be achieved in such a manner. I am personally convinced that this is the same basic epistemology that gave rise to the misplaced conviction of some nine hundred souls who followed the late Jim Jones to Jonestown, Guyana, in 1978, where they ultimately committed suicide by drinking cyanide-laced, grape, Flavor Aid. The key to this handy system of epistemology is to convince the follower to abandon the intellectual process of reasoned evaluation as an essential part of the appropriate validation of truth, and to encourage the synaptic firings of feeling based memory traces associated with anticipation of something good that is desired. It's an emotional based sales job. Every marketing executive in America knows the game and makes his living by the skill with which he employs it.

Now, while we're on the subject of confusing emotional based bias with thoughtful consideration, I recognize that there will be many who immediately feel quite "put off" with any analogy between the false prophet, Jim Jones, and the Mormon phenomena, simply on the basis of the clear differences between the "fruits" of the differing movements. The Mormons contribute to considerable good in the world. This is unquestionable. Ostensibly, they are quite "squared away" folks with relatively high moral values and many examples of successes to boast of in the world. Jim Jones' followers, on the other hand, self-destructed in a tragic mass suicide of historic proportions. I am suggesting that the difference between the two social phenomena is not found in the fundamentals of epistemology. It is found in the direction the leadership decided to take the group, once having achieved their submissive, relatively blind, obedience.

It seems reasonable to surmise that Jim Jones was a man whose own self interests, which became self destructive, were a much higher value for him than any other lofty or noble purpose. He quickly turned the power of obedience that he acquired from his followers to his own corrupt and self destructive purposes. The Mormon leadership in general, on the other hand, has, for the most part, an apparent legacy of nobility in purpose that continues today and is, for whatever critics may say about the Church, quite impressive. They continue to direct the submissive obedience that they have acquired from their followers into strong family and moral values, meaningful business and academic contributions, and civic leadership that is, at times, inspirational. For whatever occasional departures from this norm that may arise, many agree that there seems little apparent question that the simple goodness of the Mormon social track record outweighs the occasional Mormon blunders. This is not an accident, neither is it due to the "correctness" of their epistemology. It is a simple matter of noble leadership over the long haul. As a result of this leadership Mormons are, generally speaking, comparatively good people. Obediently so, submissively so.

Mormons celebrate submissiveness as an indication of spirituality and worthiness. The often quoted words of the *Book of Mormon* prophet, King Benjamin, bring the authority of "ancient" Mormon scripture to bear on the requirement that members submit willingly to the will of the Lord as it manifests itself through His priesthood leaders.

> For the natural man is an enemy to God, and has been from the fall of Adam, and will be, forever and ever, unless he yields to the enticings of the Holy Spirit, and putteth off the natural man and becometh a saint through the atonement of Christ the Lord, and becometh as a child, submissive, meek, humble, patient, full of love, willing to submit to all things which the Lord seeth fit to inflict upon him, even as a child doth submit to his father. (*Book of*

Mormon, The Book of Mosiah. Compare to page 153 of the 1981 edition)

What the Lord sees fit to "inflict" upon the members of the Mormon Church will often be preceded by a telephone call from the executive secretary to a Mormon Bishopric, informing the member that he or she has been "invited" to meet with the Bishop or a Bishop's Counselor. Mormons are expected to accept the "callings" of the Bishopric as callings of the Lord, Himself. The Mormon culture requires that the rank and file male priesthood members of the Church submit freely to the "counsel" and direction of the local Bishop, and that the Bishops submit unwaveringly to direction of their supervising ecclesiastical authorities. Wives are expected to submit to the direction of their husbands. The first law and principle of the "gospel", as presented in the Mormon temples, is obedience. Unwavering obedience is evaluated in the consideration of candidates for advancement in the priesthood. Mormonism is a culture of submissive obedience to religious authority.

I think if the Mormon leadership sent out a world-wide bulletin instructing that the sacrament should be laced with cyanide, on a given Sunday, with some contrived noble reason provided within the context of the reassuring representation that this was ordained by God in a recent revelation, the tragedy of Jonestown would become historically insignificant by comparison to the outcome. Of course, I doubt this will ever happen. The Mormon leadership is not only ostensibly noble, but it has also been established with certain checks and balances. If, on the other hand, the Mormon leadership decided, for instance, that gay marriage was an affront to God's divine plan for families, the political force of the Mormon constituency who "desired to believe" to the point of deep personal conviction would manifest itself astoundingly. And so it has, in the form of the "individual" activism expected of Mormons in the national campaign against gay marriage. Since others share this belief about God's divine plan, as it relates to gay marriage, the political ramifications of the Mormon involvement on this subject have, while clearly noticed, not actually been understood for their full political significance. Homophobia continues to abound in our society, so Mormons find some measure of shelter and support for their activism among others groups. At some point, perhaps, the Mormon leadership will see God's divine plan to require of the Mormon constituency a somewhat more socially challenging resolve. Or, then, maybe not. God's interest in polygamy was apparently abandoned when it became an obstacle to Utah's statehood and God's aversion to Blacks being called to the Mormon Priesthood was somehow placated at a time when such a position was becoming a public embarrassment. The Mormon Church, however, in those days, was clearly a religious minority struggling to outgrow its reputation as a "cult". Today, the Mormon religion has achieved political "critical mass". It is now a social and political force to be reckoned with like never before, and, some would argue, like few others. Omniscience, after all, would clearly include political savvy.

Mitt Romney, a notable Mormon High Priest who made an admirable showing of giving the late Ted Kennedy a run for his Senate seat in Massachusetts, ran on a "pro-choice" platform. He was morally opposed to abortion, but, I surmise, thought freedom of choice was consistent with the Mormon theology on the importance of the "free agency of man". Massachusetts, of course, does not have an overwhelming population of Mormon voters. It does have a significant population of liberal democrats. Subsequently, in a national bid for the republican presidential nomination, the same Mormon High Priest had an epiphany on the subject of abortion, the new basis for which still somewhat unclear to me other than its consistency with the attitude of the majority of Mormon voters on the subject. His platform then shifted to "pro-life". If historical patterns are a clue, it would seem unlikely that God will inspire the Mormon leadership with any tremendously socially or politically challenging revelations any time soon, but you never know. Who knows the mind of God, other than, of course, his exclusive agency on earth, the Mormons?

Let's get back to the ostensible historical nobility of the Mormon leadership and the good works of the Church as they relate to the epistemology of the Church. Many will make what I will call the "by the fruits" epistemological argument. There is somewhat of a Biblical basis for this. Of course, that would lead purely objective intellectual evaluators to the question of why the Bible should be considered a sound basis for anything. Mormons, who presume the Bible to be the "word of God insofar as it is translated correctly", a caveat giving rise to the need for the *Joseph Smith Translation* of the Bible, take comfort that the "by the fruits you will know them" epistemological argument is found in the 7th Chapter of Matthew, in the *New Testament*.

Actually, an attentive student of philosophy might point out that the "by the fruits" argument is more of a logical argument than an epistemological argument, and not a very strong one at that. The passage in Matthew points out that "false prophets" will be easily identifiable by their "evil fruits". By reverse inference, it is largely accepted, by Mormons, that the "good fruits" of the Church's notable efforts over the long haul should be seen to be strong clues as to the divinity of its leadership, if not conclusive evidence. The significance of this argument, and the Bible passage promoting it, is not lost on the Mormon leadership, being comprised largely of very successful retired businessmen. The Mormon Church takes great care to involve itself in good works. This is a matter of specific Mormon theology as well. Good works are required of Mormons by edict in their own uniquely canonized book of scripture known as the *Doctrine and Covenants*. Jim Jones, on the other hand, was apparently preoccupied with other things, and missed the significance of this biblical passage as it might have cast a shadow on his leadership. Unfortunately, as seen in the Jonestown tragedy, identifying a false prophet by his evil fruit might, for some less astute observers, be a methodology a little wanting in the timeliness of its relevance. Still, for all of Jim Jones' tragic flaws, talking nine hundred people into following you to a foreign country is a remarkable feat of influence. Certainly not ranking with the accomplishment of talking fifty thousand into two years of dedicated missionary service, year after year, for decades, but still quite impressive. Many of us struggle with the ongoing challenge to convince a few people that we are "ok" to "hang around" once in a while.

Even though it is true, that a bright philosophy student might call the "good fruit" argument a relatively weak one, it still remains a fact that what I will call the "good fruit phenomena" is enormously significant in Mormon epistemology. The "good fruit phenomena" has more to do with the good feelings that follow the "good fruit". In the closing chapter of the *Book of Mormon*, the concluding prophet, Moroni, wraps up his testimony of the truthfulness of the book and makes a promise that most every Mormon is intimately familiar with. His promise is in reference to the writings in the book itself. Moroni says,

> And when ye shall receive these things, I would exort you that ye would ask God the Eternal Father, in the name of Christ, if these things are not true; and if ye shall ask with a sincere heart, with real intent, having faith in Christ, he will manifest the truth of it unto you, by the power of the Holy Ghost. And by the power of the Holy Ghost ye may know the truth of all things. (*Book of Mormon, The Book of Moroni.* Compare to page 529 of the 1981 edition)

This particular scripture may well be the most quoted, by Mormon missionaries, to investigators of the Mormon Church together with certain paraphrased quotes of a scriptural verse from the Mormon canonized book of scripture called the *Doctrine and Covenants*. In one of the earlier sections of the *Doctrine and Covenants* God explains to a would-be translator of the *Book of Mormon,* through Joseph Smith, the methodology of spiritual confirmation of truth, or knowledge, saying,

> ... but behold, I say unto you, that you must study it out in your mind; then you must ask me if it be right, and if it is right I will cause that your bosom shall burn within you; therefore you shall feel that it is right. (*Doctrine & Covenants, Section 9.* Compare to page 16 of the 1981 edition)

Investigators of the Mormon Church and, in fact, all members of the Mormon Church are taught, early on, and continually reminded, that the process by which God confirms truth to the soul is through a feeling brought on by the Holy Ghost. The feeling, in particular, is a "burning in the bosom", or warmth in the heart. This feeling of warmth and comfort is pervasively the "go-to" method of epistemology employed throughout the Church, and particularly by the priesthood. It is the accepted method by which theories and proposals are confirmed by God to be seen as "true". This confirming spiritual manifestation of truth is the method by which church callings, including full time missions, are recognized as appropriate for members by priesthood leaders. It is the method by which the Mormon Church's Quorum of Twelve Apostles ratifies the revelations of the Prophet, including both the onset and termination of the practice of polygamy, and the inclusion of Blacks in eligibility for priesthood office. It is the method by which a Mormon Bishop ascertains the truth of a member's professed worthiness to attend the temple. There are countless volumes of Church literature dedicated to this very subject matter. It is the recommended method by which members of the Church select mates; careers; from paths of escape, when they are lost in the woods; who to believe in a dispute; and the appropriateness of public policy. While arguments will differ on whether or not this method is valued above empirical or other compelling evidence, when available in considering the truth of a matter, it is my own personal experience, in the Church, that the degree to which this method is employed, instead of thoughtful consideration of available factual data which is sometimes viewed dismissively in the alternative, is unnerving. It is a simple matter of truth that far too many men who profess spirituality and spiritual authority commonly get carried away in their pride, and arrogantly consider their own divine powers of intuitive revelation more reliable than concrete proof that would slap them in the face if they would be humble enough to let it. I have come to believe that professed spirituality and spiritual authority are among the most common forms of arrogance. They masquerade as humility before God while serving the egos and agendas of their hosts.

I, personally, sat in the presence of a General Authority of the Church of Jesus Christ of Latter Day Saints, at his own invitation, having expressed an interest in concerns I had about inappropriate conduct in the priesthood. I listened to him brag about ten thousand members he had preached repentance to, and sent on their way, arrogantly finding no need to consider their concerns, or my concerns, beyond a superficial level. We all just needed to repent. He told me so, on behalf of God. He made his speech. I was apparently number ten thousand and one, and he did not appear to have any interest in any discussion that ran any deeper than "cleansing his garments" from my sinful questions about priesthood conduct by declaring his testimony to me that I needed to repent. I understood that this was the man that had supervisory authority over mission calls for the entire Church at the time of the aforementioned unpaid alimony fiasco. Whether this was actually his particular responsibility or not, he professed to have joint responsibility with all officers of the Church for the conduct of the priesthood. Such is consistent with Mormon doctrine on the subject of the priesthood. He didn't take time beyond a cursory level to explore my concerns. That, apparently, wasn't worth the investment of his time. The professed interest in my concern, as it turned out, seemed to be just a ruse to get me into his office so he could tell me I needed to repent, as was clearly apparent, since I had questions about the integrity of the priesthood. I'm sure others had told him of my alleged sins and need for repentance, and their representations were, no doubt, complimented by his own "feelings" that they were true, amidst the clear evidence that I presumed to question the appropriateness of the conduct of ordained officers of the Church. What became immediately clear was that his innuendos about certain of my particular "sins" were made with a considerable degree of comfort while he, apparently, had no inclination whatsoever to afford me any direct information as to the substance of exactly what I had been accused of, nor by who, nor an opportunity to respond. Such, I guessed, would have been a superfluous waste of his time, given that the confirmation of my sinfulness, and its direct bearing on the legitimacy of my complaints, had already been made manifest to him by the Holy Ghost. Unfortunately, as it turned out, I was not guilty of what he particularly insinuated. I knew that I was not guilty of it, and I was very much aware that it was being insinuated by a man who professed the divine authority and the guiding Spirit of God in the process of his insinuations. I didn't realize it at the time, but it turns out he had a personal interest in raising questions about my credibility which I now understand better.

The "burning in the bosom" or "warm heart" test for validation of truth has its obvious problems, but it is still an enormously effective device in acquiring and nurturing the devotion of millions of Mormon members. You see, the Mormon Church doesn't, typically, appeal to drug dealers, or pimps, or alcoholics, or prostitutes. These are not the particular target audience to whose attention the Church's missionary force of more than fifty thousand is primarily directed. The Church seeks out young single moms, newlyweds, new home owners, survivors of the recently deceased, and parents of newborns, among other special groups, not that anyone else would be turned away. There is a reason for this. People who fall into these particular categories are the most likely to be at a place in their lives where they recall, with longing, the comfort of hearth and home, and have an intense desire to share the best of what they remember about their childhood experiences with their families. These are people who long for the synaptic triggering of those familiar memory traces associated with the anticipation of the comfort and security that they, subconsciously, have connected with mom from their infancy. With such people, the Mormon conversion process becomes quite simple. Trigger the anticipation while promoting an epistemology that skips the intellectual process. These people experience intense feelings of comfort upon being accompanied to beautiful chapels with well manicured lawns and filled with young families with shiny cars and pearly white teeth. They are "taken in" by the attention given to family values, and fidelity in marriage, and financial security. It is quite understandable that they have very intense desires to believe that this is the answer to their anxieties about life. They easily come to believe that such values are the answers to their anxieties about life. After all, for the most part, such is true about these values. They are the answers to many of the anxieties about life. So they, quite understandably, feel deep feelings of comfort and harmony amidst their new friends. Their hearts are warmed. They are now primed for the pivotal doctrinal lesson of the Church.

The most significant and key message of the Church, at this point, is now impressed upon them by many new friends who know the curriculum like the back of their hand. Prospective members find themselves surrounded by new friends, all of whom are well familiar with the critical timing of the moment and the needed content of their messages. Paraphrasing, the speech goes something like this, "Those feelings that you feel, those heartwarming feelings, they are spoken of by ancient prophets. They are the manifestations of the Holy Ghost, confirming to your soul that: the *Book of Mormon* is true; that Joseph Smith was a prophet of God; that Jesus Christ lives and guides and directs this Church through a modern day Prophet, who leads our Church today; and that God lives, and loves you, and has directed you to this discovery and to our nurturing fellowship. There is no need for further consideration of these matters. The truth of these things has been confirmed to your soul by the power of the Holy Ghost." To devout members of the Mormon Church, this epistemology is as fundamental to their life as the air they breathe. When the Star Wars hero, Luke Skywalker, was told to abandon his computer assisted targeting device and "trust the force", Mormons knew he was a true hero. This is the Mormon "fix". It has everything to do with the Mormon epistemology. If you can be convinced to suspend the intellectual process of careful evaluation of all relevant facts and trust your heart, you will easily find your way to believe what you desire to believe in anticipation of the warmth and security of hearth and home. It works because so much of it is consistent with the reality of life, already experienced at the subconscious level by the convert, from infancy. It is very difficult for many to control their emotional desire to believe and embrace what they want so desperately to be true. Not too many people even want to control their emotional desire to believe. Why should they? What's the harm? A lot worse mistakes than joining a group of people devoted to such values are made in life, particularly a group with such a seemingly consistent track record of continuity, in the support of those values, over the long haul. What is easily overlooked in the process of this spiritual infatuation, is a simple sociological reality that becomes harder and harder for Mormons to consider. This reality is that good people who may be right about a lot of things aren't necessarily right about everything. What is overlooked is that the sublime, harmonious spirit, so commonly associated with the Mormon experience, is so sublime because of the values that they collectively devote themselves to. People who aspire to goodness and decency feel naturally comfortable when surrounded by a supportive group of people who share those values. That will always be true about society, whether Joseph Smith was a Prophet or not, and whether the *Book of Mormon* is true or not.

One of the more common and successful marketing practices in business is the practice of "bundling". Savvy retailers and distributors bundle packages of products and services for "discount" prices that are less than what the retail "a la carte" price for each of the products or services in the bundle would be. In this way, hotter products with more market demand can be bundled with products with lower comparative market demand, thereby helping the retailer move products that he might not be able to sell so easily or profitably on their own. Most of us have had the experience of making a purchase of a bundle of products or services that included things that we had no interest in, on the basis of the argument that, on balance, the overall value of the bundle was worth the asking price, because what we did want was acquired as part of a reasonably priced package.

The Mormon bundled package deal includes the hot commodities of a meaningful support system for the pursuit of family continuity; apparent stability and financial security; opportunities for meaningful and heartwarming service to one's fellow man; and, in the fine print, acceptance of the Church of Jesus Christ of Latter Day Saints as the sole agency on the earth authorized to receive, interpret, and communicate God's will to you, which, let's be clear; begins immediately with the requirement of ten percent of your annual earnings turned over to the Church, and the dedication of whatever time it takes to serve in the callings that may be required of you, and your submission to the Mormon Priesthood generally. It is hoped that the intense anticipation of the benefits of the first parts of the bundle will give rise to such a strong desire to believe that thoughtful consideration of the last part will be overlooked as an unnecessary intellectual exercise. After all, the Holy Ghost already confirmed the truth of the bundle, just like those ancient *Book of Mormon* prophets predicted they would. And, "gosh", who could doubt them? They "nailed" the whole thing about the restoration of the Church through a prophet named Joseph in these "Latter Days"! How handy is that?

For those prospective members of the Church who are inclined toward a more vicarious heartwarming experience, the *Book of Mormon* provides a fabulous epic saga that leaves many readers with a strong desire to believe it is true. One notable exception, of course, would be the famous author of *Tom Sawyer* and *Huckleberry Fin*, Samuel Clemens, whose pen name was Mark Twain. Samuel Clemens has been quoted as saying he thought the *Book of Mormon* was "chloroform in print". For the benefit of younger readers, chloroform was used in the practice of medicine, as a general anesthesia to put people to sleep. Apparently, Samuel Clemens thought the *Book of Mormon* was quite boring. We might consider that he was a fiction writer, and he probably read the *Book of Mormon* as a fiction.

The *Book of Mormon* is presented to investigators of the Mormon Church as an authentic record of ancient prophets who lived on the American continent. With the heightened mystique of being an actual collection of the diaries of real prophets from ancient times, the book is significantly more impactful. It is routinely presented to non-Mormon friends, by members of the Church, with their handwritten testimony as to its veracity and authenticity as just such an ancient prophetic record. This testimony, of course, would be based on the application of Moroni's aforementioned promise, and Alma's epistemology, which is thoughtfully recommended to the prospect. Sincere folks that they are, the testimonies of the solicitous Mormon friends are usually enough to get the prospect into at least the first few pages of a book that might not have, otherwise, seemed compelling enough to open at all. In those first few pages, the ancient Prophet, Nephi, introduces himself as Lehi's son, and goes right into a story of intrigue, mystical dreams, and homicide, with a curious justification that would not work in today's courts but somehow appeals to Mormons. Many readers make it through the "historical record" of ancient civilizations that fell in and out of favor with God. Obedience to God's commandments, as communicated by His prophets, is the over-riding message, reinforced by the scary examples of what happens to the disobedient and heartwarming examples of what happens to the obedient. The majority of the book makes up the back story for its crucial and pivotal point. This is the single point on which the entire Mormon faith rests. It is not, as the Church has in more recent times attempted to convey with a significant marketing focus, the point that Jesus is the Christ. Clearly, the book does purport to confirm that message about Jesus. However, neither the existence, nor the divinity of Jesus Christ necessarily gives rise to the need for the formal organization of the Mormon Church, nor its claim that any previous baptism of a candidate for membership would not be valid for lack of the Mormon priesthood authority. What makes the *Book of Mormon* so key to the Mormon faith and integral to the Mormon doctrine, is that the *Book of Mormon* "foretells" the "restoration" of the priesthood authority of Jesus Christ through the "Latter Day" Prophet who would be named Joseph; and further explains that obedience to God's commandments, as continually revealed by and through His prophets, is required for exaltation in the Kingdom of God. That's the "gotcha" that makes the *Book of Mormon* a "cornerstone" of the Mormon faith. In short, by divine decree of ancient Prophets, the Mormon Church lays claim to the benefit of your free time for service in their Church, as they see fit, and the collection of your tithing. Not some other Christian Church. Of all of the "plain and precious truths" supposedly lost from the Bible, that the *Book of Mormon* is supposed to restore, that is the real salient point of the *Book of Mormon*. I contend that there is no other. The Mormon Church will, of course, have another view. Fortunately, this salient message is enveloped in heartwarming accounts of God's love and blessings to the faithful, that give rise to a significant desire to believe, in many readers, which is, predictably, reaffirmed to the prayerful reader by the power of the Holy Ghost, just like the concluding prophet, Moroni, foretells. The *Book of Mormon* stories really are quite touching, if taken seriously. I must admit that I felt a profound sense of heartwarming gratification when I read it, as a young man. I was convinced that I had received a manifestation of the truthfulness of the *Book of Mormon,* just like Moroni predicted. Of course, I had been reading the *Book of Mormon* for weeks on end, and was praying fervently for just such a manifestation, as required by the Mormon epistemological formula, so my spiritual manifestation was relatively assured.

I have come to realize that the heartwarming feelings that I once believed to be manifestations of the Holy Ghost, confirming to me that the *Book of Mormon* and the Mormon Church were true, were actually just the naturally occurring phenomena resulting from talking one's self into feeling a "spiritual" manifestation. I was a young man, who fervently wanted to be blessed with a spiritual manifestation of the truthfulness of the Church, as Moroni promised. I fixated on that desire until it became true for me. There is really nothing at all remarkable about this. What is remarkable is that millions of people, world-wide, either can't or won't see it for what it really is. The desire to believe is one of the most compelling forces in the world. It is easily harnessed by those who seize upon the opportunity to assume a leadership role over those who are only too happy to believe and subordinate.

It was explained to me once, by a General Authority of the Church, that the power of a man's, or an institution's, priesthood can be measured by the obedience acquired by that man, or institution, from souls, without compulsory means. By this standard, the Mormon priesthood is, perhaps, the most powerful in the world. However, I sincerely believe that the true power of this priesthood flows from the faith of the people, upward. It has much to do with the general nobility with which the Mormon leadership manages this power. I now believe it has nothing to do with the divinity of that power. The notion of this divinity, however, raises other interesting questions.

At this point, I should point out that I do not argue that the existence of an alternative practical explanation for the development of faith, and certain feelings associated with the identification of truth, as a natural pattern of human development should necessarily be seen to rule out other explanations. I am often annoyed by the notion that something can be disproved by identifying a practical alternative explanation for occurrences attributed to it. Such is not necessarily the case. A closer examination of the Mormon theology on the subject of the Holy Ghost, and manifestations of truth associated with the Holy Ghost, is worthwhile and enlightening, and should be considered in the spirit of objectivity.

Mormons believe in a Godhead consisting of three distinct personages. First and foremost, they recognize as God, the Eternal Father. Jesus Christ and the Holy Ghost make up the other two members of the Godhead, for Mormons. Unlike many other Christians, the Mormons do not believe that Jesus Christ, or the Holy Ghost, are simply alternative manifestations of the same God. They actually believe that the three personages exist apart from each other, and function in distinct and separate roles, all of which are meaningful and necessary in their own right. According to Mormon theology, the manifestation, or confirmation, of truth, in the form of a heartwarming or spiritual feeling, is actually a spiritual confirmation of truth that has much to do with the actual spiritual and physical realities of our existence, and relationship with the Godhead. The Mormon theology about this relationship is based largely on the teaching of the Mormon Prophet, Joseph Smith, and his interpretations of the Bible, combined with his own "revelations", the most officially accepted of which being compiled in the Mormon canonized book of scripture called the *Doctrine and Covenants,* and finally, on the teachings found in the *Book of Mormon.* A brief explanation of the theology follows. It is, in my opinion, quite beautiful and sublime. I don't think it would be unlikely that some readers will "feel" that it is true.

Chapter 4

The Plan of Salvation

Fundamental to the Mormon belief in God's "Plan of Salvation", for all mankind, is what they believe to be the true identity, attributes, and roles of the three members of the Godhead, and our relationship to each member of the Godhead. The Mormon belief about the Godhead, as well as all of the Mormon beliefs, are rooted in the teachings of the founding Mormon prophet, Joseph Smith, as found in his own personal published revelations and interpretation of the Bible. In explaining the Mormon theology regarding the Plan of Salvation, I will forego some scriptural references and historical quotes. It is not my purpose to document the bibliography or origins of the theology, or to argue in favor of its Biblical correctness. I am simply setting forth the basic theology, as a basis for understanding the Mormon belief about the process by which truth is revealed, or confirmed, to mankind.

Mormons believe that God, "the Eternal Father", often referred to by Mormons as "Heavenly Father", is the supreme being of the universe, and literal spiritual father of all of humanity, that does now, ever has, or ever will live on this earth or other worlds. To understand this, it is useful to understand the Mormon concept of the soul of mankind. According to the *Doctrine and Covenants*, the spirit and mortal body of man, together, make up his soul. (*Doctrine & Covenants, Section 88.* Compare to page 16 of the 1981 edition.) In the interest of brevity, please assume now, and hereafter, that each reference to "man", in the context of this discussion, includes both man and woman. I apologize to any feminists who prefer that I refer to both collectively as "woman". It is, after all, Mormon theology that we are discussing here.

While most people believe that the mortal body of man is a material reality, Mormons believe that the spirit is also made of "finer or purer" matter, as well, and can be "discerned with purer eyes". (*Doctrine & Covenants, Section 131.* Compare to page 266 of the 1981 edition.) Separately, the intelligence of man has been defined in a variety of ways, including the "light of truth". (*Doctrine & Covenants, Section 93.* Compare to page 182 of the 1981 edition.) Each of the components of the soul of man has a somewhat different origin. The intelligence of man "was not created or made, neither indeed can be" according to the *Doctrine and Covenants.* (*Doctrine & Covenants, Section 93.* Compare to page 182 of the 1981 edition.) This particular element of our identity, according to Mormon theology, always existed. In a pre-earthly existence, the Mormons believe that our spirits were "begotten" of God. As such, Mormons believe that we are, literally, the spiritual offspring of God, and lived in His presence in a spiritual state of existence prior to the beginning of our sojourn on this earth, in our mortal bodies. While in this spiritual state of pre-mortal existence, the Mormon theology holds that we experienced the presence of God the Eternal Father, who was not limited to a spiritual state, but rather, was a complete "glorified and perfected" soul. This would have included His intelligence, spirit, and physical body, in a "glorified and perfected" state of existence. As such, God was, and is, omnipotent (all powerful), and omniscient (all knowing). Mormons believe that the "glory of God is intelligence, or, in other words, light and truth". There is not an overwhelming abundance of publicly distributed material making official doctrinal declarations of the Church on the subject of the omnipotence of God, so I have taken some liberties with my own interpretations and understanding as follows: The power of God emanates from, or is manifested in the application of an intelligent and volitional focus of energy in an anticipated outcome or objective. Some may argue that God no longer acts in faith, because he has a perfect knowledge of all things. On the other hand, Joseph Smith declared that "the principle of power which existed in the bosom of God, by which he framed the worlds, was faith". (Joseph Smith, Jr., 1805-1844. Compare to *Lectures on Faith, First Lecture,* delivered during 1834 and 1835 to the "School of the Prophets" at Kirkland, Ohio.) Joseph Smith also declared that "faith is the moving cause of all action in temporal concerns, so it is in spiritual." (Compare to *Lectures on Faith, First Lecture*) So it would seem that according to the Mormon theology, the omnipotence of God had much to do with the faith of God. I would argue, as I have argued earlier, that at the particular point in which the knowledge, or belief, that a given outcome will result from a particular application of energy, is sufficient to motivate one to take action on that belief, or knowledge, in order to bring about the anticipated outcome, faith has been made manifest. Faith is the emergence of applied energy that is motivated by knowledge, or belief, in an anticipated outcome. Faith is the phenomena that is made manifest when an awareness of certain realities, that are understood to have a relationship to an anticipated outcome, and a desire for that outcome, give rise to the volitional action of applied energy to the outcome. To know something will occur under certain circumstances, or to believe that it will occur, is not to contribute to its occurrence. Neither knowledge, nor belief, contributes to any outcome, without intelligently focused volitional action taken in anticipation of the outcome. Thus, the omniscience of God does not alone account for His omnipotence. The omnipotence of God comes from the convergence of His intelligence, or omniscience, and His volitional will to purposefully harness and focus energy. It, perhaps, goes without saying, that God's knowledge of how to harness and focus energy purposefully, without destroying Himself, with that energy, is not irrelevant to His immortality and continued existence and omnipotence. We, on the other hand, as mortals, have a hard time getting out of our own way, as it were. We are constantly bungling into various forms of self destruction, as we haphazardly apply our increasing, but limited, knowledge of the realities that surround us to serve our own desires, pleasures, and egos.

As romantic and allegorical as this theology sounds, I believe that it also happens to be consistent, on some very interesting levels, with certain physical realities of the universe as we are discovering them. We know that light can be converted into magnificent power through magnification and focus which is best achieved in an environment of a sort of atomic harmony. We are also coming to understand that our very awareness as human beings or, in some respects, our intelligence, is largely a manifestation of harmonious electromagnetic impulses of energy, and that the expansion of our intelligence is best achieved when we are in a state of harmony with realities that we come to know of.

Now, given that Mormons believe that our very spirits were made up of finer matter, and that we had intelligence, or the "light of truth", it follows that the presence of God's glorified and perfected soul would have had a powerful and very real impact on the finer matter of our spirits and intelligences, at the atomic level, in our pre-earthly state, as we experienced this presence. I think it reasonably follows, that the electromagnetic force of God's presence would have had an enormous impact on our spiritual selves, and left us with a certain physical attraction or recognition of that force, in the same sense that a pin becomes magnetized when left in the presence of a powerful magnet. The atoms of the two objects naturally harmonize their energy. The greater naturally drawing the lesser into harmony with the realities of its own existence. Examples of this are seen in the reality of the physical universe in which we live. Whether we believe in God or not, this is the reality of electromagnetic energy. As such, it is basic to the Mormon theology that our spirits acquired a sensitivity for truth or "light", while in the presence of God, that would be carried into this next life with us, resulting in the ability to feel a certain confirmation of truth, at the spiritual or, in other words, atomic or finer matter level.

Understandably imprinted, according to the Mormon theology, in the pre-mortal soul of man, from experiencing the presence of God, is the desire to progress to the state of becoming like God. Mormons believe, as taught by the fifth president of the Mormon Church, Lorenzo Snow, "as man is, God once was" and "as God is, man may become." (Conference address, June 1840) This is fundamental to the Mormon paradigm of life and eternity. Devout Mormons believe that this quest for "Eternal" or "Celestial" life is the most important quest. It is the quest to become like God. Mormons believe that a God-like state is achievable in the "life after death" for all who qualify for a continuation of "eternal progress" by conformity in their lives, through obedience to revealed truth, while in this mortal life. Such conformity, it is believed, unleashes, for devout Mormons, additional revelations of truth and additional opportunities for the application of faith. In this way, it is believed that the mortal existence of man is an absolutely necessary step in becoming like God. We must acquire physical bodies, and we must acquire and perfect the application of our faith as we pursue increasing intelligence. The development of faith, if properly pursued along with the pursuit of intelligence, should increase our volitional power. The will to assess, surmise, calculate, and then take intelligent action in anticipation of a desired result, without the experience based knowledge of the surety of the desired outcome, is precisely the particular personal strength and power that we seek in our effort to become empowered as human beings, and ultimately to become like God. I would be surprised if Anthony Robbins, the notable success guru, would argue with the process, as it relates to the achievement of personal goals of any kind. Mormons believe that this developmental process is the very purpose of our sojourn on this earth. They believe that the developmental objective requires a physical body, through which we experience more completely the realities of the universe. This plan also, according to the Mormon theology, required that a veil of forgetfulness be placed over our minds, upon entry into this mortal existence, so that we would be left largely dependant on the development of experience based intelligence and faith in order to survive and progress, as opposed to a vivid recollection of our pre-mortal life in God's presence.

Just as it would seem impractical and unfair to expect an infant to figure its own way out in the world, without guidance along the way, the Mormon theology holds that God has not left us without guidance in this earthly sojourn. The veil of forgetfulness was necessary, so that we would be required to make our way through life by exercising and developing faith, but it was seen as equally necessary that certain basic truths be revealed to the children of "Heavenly Father" on this earth, as they are prepared to receive them. These truths would be revealed through appropriately appointed Prophets. We would recognize these prophets to be true prophets of God, as opposed to false prophets, and these truths to be true, by the power of the Holy Ghost. This process would consist of a core feeling, or sense of recognition of the truths, at a personal level, being validated, or re-affirmed, by an additional and stronger sense or feeling of truth, characterized as a "burning in the bosom", brought on by a manifestation of the Holy Ghost. The particular role of the Holy Ghost, in Mormon theology, is precisely this.

Mormons believe that the purpose of God, as it relates to humankind, is "to bring to pass [their] immortality and eternal life". (*Pearl of Great Price, Selections from the Book of Moses.* Compare to page 4 of the 1981 edition.) Immortality is understood to be a state of ongoing life without death. Eternal life, on the other hand, is a quality of life, like that of God. An eternal life, in the Mormon theology, is a life that would be characterized by omnipotence, omniscience, and immortality. One final and additional characteristic of eternal life is significant to Mormons. Arguably, for some, it is the most significant aspect of eternal life. It is the continuation of family life and power to procreate. Mormons believe that extended families will continue in their family relationships throughout the eternities, for those souls who qualify for celestial or eternal life. They also believe that qualifying "celestial" souls will have the ability to beget spiritual offspring, and populate their own worlds. They do not believe that other, non-qualifying souls, even those who are otherwise "saved", will enjoy a continuation of family relationships, or even the power to procreate. Only those who qualify for celestial glory, or eternal life, do. Souls who do not qualify for the Celestial Kingdom of glory are relegated to lesser kingdoms of glory. A very significant difference between the Celestial Kingdom and lesser kingdoms, in Mormon theology, is the continuation of eternal progressive development. Eternal progress continues for those who qualify for the Celestial Kingdom. Those who only qualify for lesser kingdoms will, according to Mormon theology, never progress beyond those lesser kingdoms, and are in that way "damned". To Mormons, "damnation" is not to be relegated to a certain physical place, where ongoing physical torment occurs, but rather, to be limited for the rest of eternity, by the natural bounds created as a result of one's own lack of demonstrated discipline, intelligence, and faith. Damnation, then, is not so much what one is assigned, but rather, what one chooses, by virtue of what they have become.

Qualifying for eternal life, is understood to be a process of spiritual development achieved through obedience to truth, as it is progressively revealed to the individual, "line upon line", and "precept upon precept". (*Doctrine & Covenants, Section 98*. Compare to page 190 of the 1981 edition.) Participation in certain covenant based ordinances is believed to evidence this progress, as it is achieved through obedience. These ordinances are also believed to unlock an increase in spiritual harmony with truth, for the individual, which progressively results in manifestations of greater and more advanced truths, to the individual. These covenant based ordinances are only considered to be valid if administered by appropriate priesthood officiators. The ordinances begin with baptism, and include participation in weekly sacraments. Ultimately, the higher or more advanced ordinances are administered in the Mormon temples only to members who have demonstrated a "base line" of worthiness to enter the temple. The ultimate or most advanced ordinance administered by Mormon priesthood officiators in the temples is the "sealing" of a man and a wife in an "eternal marriage". (*Doctrine & Covenants, Section 131*. Compare to page 266 of the 1981 edition.) Mormons believe that their priesthood officiators have the special "keys" and authority to seal a couple together on earth, in a marriage that will survive through the eternities, assuming each party to the marriage continues faithfully and obediently to honor their various covenants up to and including those which are a part of that marriage. All children born under the covenant of that special sealing ordinance of marriage are automatically sealed to the parents, for "all time and eternity". These sealings are believed to be valid beyond the "veil" and into the next life, by virtue of God's priesthood authority vested in the temple officiators, for those members of the Church who remain faithful to their covenants. The sealing is broken by the sinner who breaks his temple covenants and fails to repent and get back on track. Such are disqualified for celestial life in the hereafter, and disjoined from the eternal families. They become immortal bachelors or bachelorettes. For those who might be tempted, upon looking over at their aging spouse, to consider that being single might be more desirable than celestial life, we are reminded that the celestial bodies will be restored to the prime of their life. That may be a helpful incentive for some.

With the understanding of this overall Plan of Salvation in mind, it can be seen that the Mormon's larger paradigm of life considers the greater context of their view of the pre-existence, and the life after death, and the relationship that choices in this life will have through the eternities. The spiritual sensitivity for truth brought into this life coupled with the complimentary manifestations of the Holy Ghost make up the method by which Mormons believe they can expect to navigate their way back to the Celestial Kingdom in the next life. Recognizing truth, in the proscribed way, is the key. Every devout Mormon will search their heart for an understanding of truth. All too many, unfortunately, will rely on feelings to the exclusion of rational processing of relevant information or facts.

Chapter 5

The Merits of Scrutiny

As romantic an allegory as God's Plan of Salvation is, according to Mormon theology, it is not altogether unique to Mormonism. Certain elements of this system of beliefs about the various stages of existence of our souls are found in other religions, faiths, and cultures. In its entirety, it is unique to the Mormon faith. Mormons will argue that this is due to their exclusive channel of continuing revelation from God, being His only authorized priesthood agents on earth, for the purpose of revealing this plan to the world and administering the ordinances that it requires in this mortal existence to those who are willing and worthy. This Plan of Salvation is not presented by the Mormon Church as an allegory, but rather an absolute reality of eternal existence that gives rise to the essential role that the Mormon priesthood must play in the lives of all of humanity. Clearly, such a claim warrants scrutiny for those who are seriously considering a life commitment on this basis. The personal commitment that a Mormon lifestyle involves is not at all trivial, but daunting. In his *Lectures on Faith*, Joseph Smith taught, "... a religion that does not require the sacrifice of all things, never has power sufficient to produce the faith necessary unto life and salvation..." (Joseph Smith, Jr., 1805-1844. Compare to *Lectures on Faith, Lecture Sixth*) Make no mistake, once the Mormon priesthood is accepted as a fixture in the life of the member of the Church, it will readily assume its role as the exclusive agency of God, by which the sacrifices that will be required of the member are made known. Tithing is only the beginning. Let there be no doubt that the crowning temple covenant that is administered by ritual ordinance and affirmative acceptance by the member is the covenant of "consecration", by which the member is obliged to consecrate all of his life, time, talents, and all of his earthly substance to the building up the Church of Jesus Christ of Latter Day Saints. This covenant is declared, by the Mormon priesthood, to be preparatory and necessary for exaltation in the Kingdom of God. The very purpose of the entire Mormon religion, including each and every meeting, lesson, conference, or class, is to progressively move the member toward the acceptance of this ultimate covenant of "consecration".

Considerable social pressure, in the Mormon culture, is applied to overlooking an otherwise obvious reality about the human condition, in a rush for quick acceptance of a feeling based testimony that the Church's claims are true. This unpopular reality is the fallibility of human perceptions and feelings, particularly as they are complicated by memory traces, emotions, and desires. Even where one may accept the possibility of a validating feeling of truth on a soulful level, through spiritual communion and spiritual sensitivity to truth, the complexity of the human body, brain, and psyche give rise to very significant challenges in differentiating between feelings on all levels. Aside from the very real practical issues that apply to the differentiation of human feelings, that is to say, the actual feelings themselves, as opposed to what gives rise to the feelings, there are also the practical issues related to the reliability of the connections one ascribes to the actual cause of those feelings. I certainly do not join with those who take the position that such things are altogether unknowable or otherwise completely unreliable and therefore should be dismissed entirely as irrelevant to the process of differentiating truth from a hypothesis, or identifying knowledge. I suggest, however, that utmost caution should be used as we attempt to refine and develop an understanding of our own perceptions, particularly the more subjective manifestations of those perceptions, such as the feelings they give rise to. I sincerely believe, on the basis of my own personal life experience, study, and observations, that feelings alone, while potentially useful in contributing to our accurate perceptions of reality and accumulation of reliable knowledge, are altogether unreliable on their own without other methods of what I call "cross validation". It is my position, the amended position that I do now recommend to any of my progeny who might take the time to read this, and the amended position that I advocate to all with whom I ever shared my testimony of the Church, that it is vital that we continually seek other, more objective, approaches to the validation of truth with which to compliment our feelings, before accepting anything as truth, no matter how noble appearing the organization or individual that advocates the purported truth seems to be.

It is important that I acknowledge that my previous testimony was ill founded. I reject the notion that it is an alliance with Satan that gives rise to such an epiphany of self-awareness. The humility, amidst my otherwise prideful nature, that is required to admit my fallibility, has grown out of the increasing value that I place on being honest with myself, in a quest for an understanding of truth, without bias or social prejudice. Honesty in awareness of one's own fallibilities is not evil. This is a good thing. The discovery that such thoughtfulness and sincerity is so often condemned as evil, and prideful, has been very disconcerting for me. It is ironic that those who most readily condemn me as a prideful Satan follower, on the basis of this acknowledgment of my fallibility, are those who rush to declare their "knowledge" of things that are socially convenient for them to declare, in the absence of any meaningful consideration of the term "knowledge", as it should be differentiated from "belief" or "desire" or "wish". Mormons do not generally share their testimonies as to their "belief" that the Church is true, but rather their "knowledge" that it is true. Belief is not as fashionable as knowledge. The honors of the more prominent and respectable priesthood callings are not bestowed on those who are seen to believe, but rather, those who declare that they know. An epistemology discussion of the meaningful difference between the two, and the relative merits of what should be considered a sufficient basis for reclassifying a belief as a truth, or knowledge, are unwelcome at Mormon gatherings, with the exception, of course, of a dutiful acceptance of the epistemology recommended by the *Book of Mormon*. As I have come to value honesty with myself, above the accolades of my peers, I am left to wonder about this. It seems to me that any God who is represented to be God, and who is professed to have created human kind, must surely be aware of the inescapable reality of the fallibility of human perception and feelings. Such a God must also surely be aware of the corruptibility of men who aspire to represent Him, and who wish to convince others that they do, for their own selfish, egotistical, or prideful purposes. Any God, whose "work and glory" is professed to be "to bring to pass the immortality and eternal life of man", must necessarily be a God who recognizes that the eternal life of man involves the development and refinement of the intelligence of man. The Mormon Church, in particular, maintains that "the glory of God is intelligence". Any God, whose very purpose includes bringing to pass the progressive development of man's intelligence, with the ultimate eternal goal of omniscience and omnipotence in mind, cannot possibly be a God who would require of His spirit children the abdication of the intellectual process of reasoning, as an integral and essential part of the system whereby they apprehend truth and knowledge, consistent with the realities of His universe. It is my view that any Church that would advocate in whole, or in part, the abdication of the reasoning process, in favor of excessive reliance on a feeling based witness of truth, cannot be a Church that represents a God that is reasonable, just, or unchanging. It is inescapable to note, for any real student of

Christianity, that the Christian God is defined by the Christian Bible, as, among other things, "just" and "unchanging". Thus, it has been argued, that the very attributes of God are defined in such a way as to exclude Him, by definition, as the object of worship or aspiration in much, if not most, of religious practice, where that religious practice is hostile to the reasoning process. In my view, the reasoning process employs the very spark of divinity in all of us. It is through intelligence that our "God-given" faculties are made manifest in their highest and best use. It is through intelligence that we discriminate between the choices that life presents us with, selecting that which is ethical, and fair, and just, and kind. In my experience and observations in life, those who abdicate the reasoning process in deference to "feeling" based conclusions justify injustice more often than those who don't. Not less often.

Naturally, the Mormon priesthood leadership will gingerly distance itself from openly advocating the abdication of reason and scrutiny of all that is available and relevant in the process of apprehending truth. However, the *Book of Mormon* is unmistakably clear in the method by which one is expected to apprehend a conviction of the truth of its authenticity. Missionaries for the Mormon Church are trained to redirect complex or probing questions about the Church's claims, or doctrines, back to the application of Alma's epistemology and the promise of Moroni. Not only missionary training lessons but entire books have been dedicated to the subject and method of this redirection. The technique involves the careful and polite dismissal of questions of a challenging or probing nature, and redirection of the investigator's focus on the quest for a "spiritual testimony" of the *Book of Mormon*. The paradox here is that the reasoning process is applied to discourage the reasoning process. I will paraphrase a sample discussion as it has been taught to Mormon missionaries. "Mr. Jones," asks the Missionary, "wouldn't you agree with me that if the *Book of*

Mormon is true, then Joseph Smith must have been a prophet of God, and if Joseph Smith was a prophet of God, then the Church of Jesus Christ has been restored to the earth, as we have testified, and we are authorized representatives of Jesus Christ, here to share the simple truths of His gospel with you. It is not necessary that God reveal the answer to each and every question that may eventually arise, before the acceptance of His gospel by baptism. This is not the method by which God reveals the truth of his gospel to us. All answers will be revealed in the Lord's due time, as a result of the exercise of your faith. If you will follow Alma's advice, and allow a desire to believe that the Book of Mormon is true to take root in your heart, and nurture that desire with a sincere heart, you will come to know it is true, by the spiritual experience of feeling that truth swell within you. When the Holy Ghost manifests to you that the Book of Mormon is true, you can demonstrate your faith by acting on that 'witness', by trusting in the Lord and accepting baptism into His Church. Thereafter you may rely, with confidence, that the rest will fall into place and make sense. The Lord will answer all of your questions, in due time, as your faith is exercised. So, rather than pursue further discussion of your questions, Mr. Jones, we would like to invite you to read the *Book of Mormon* and ask God in sincere prayer to reveal the truth of it to you, as Moroni has promised that He will, by the confirming feeling of the Holy Ghost, bearing witness to your heart that these things are true. We testify to you, Mr. Jones, that God will reveal the truth of these things to you, in that way."

As handy as this systematic approach to simplifying the conversion process for Mr. Jones is, the unfortunate reality remains, that it undermines the most fundamentally relevant question about the very concept of truth that must be addressed as a prerequisite to identifying the criteria for its qualification.

When, in the tradition of the New Testament, Jesus found himself before the Roman procurator, Pontius Pilate, He was asked, "What is truth?" Since we understand Pilate to occupy the role of villain in this tradition, it is easy to see the question as derisive and disrespectful. Whether or not Pilate actually intended to pose the question with a spirit of mockery, in this moment, the fact remains that the question was a serious topical philosophical question of the day, to which considerable discussion and debate had been dedicated. The question has, throughout the millennia, remained among the more pivotal and key questions of diligent self reflection and philosophical inquiry. It is also, quite possibly, one of the most overlooked questions on earth. In our rush for the comfort and security of religious, political, or social alliance we have a tendency to accept as truth whatever is required of us by the group. Truth, then, is reduced, for lack of consideration, to being nothing more than what one must be seen to advocate or support in order to survive and get along socially in his chosen clique. In the case of fairly simple matters, such as the color of a shoe or directions to a store, the qualifying criterion by which truth is identified is simple consistency with known facts. This consistency is easily ascertained due to the availability of empirical and uncomplicated evidence for scrutiny. In such matters social convention for the qualification of truth is almost universal across modern cultures. In more abstract matters, the qualification of truth presents us with increasingly difficult challenges. In mathematical equations, balance is an accepted qualifying convention. This balance is dependent on acceptance of the underlying values assigned to numbers. To apprehend mathematical truth, one must first learn and accept the applicable conventions. Moral or ethical truth gives rise to additional complications. What is right? What is wrong? What makes "right" right? What makes "wrong" wrong?

Everyone alive today was born into a world where social rules purporting to be "moral" were long established by those who dominated the society into which we were born. Adherence to the rules that preceded us generally wins us the favor of our parents, or fellow man, and affords us the avoidance of punishment and isolation. Does this make those rules right? To what truth does one look to ascertain the appropriateness of a social or moral rule? Do we look to the decree of Congress? Are these men not politicians? Do we look to the school district? Are these people not bureaucrats? Some will say, "*The Bible*". Why? "Because it is the word of God", is the quick reply. Who is God? What is God? Whose God is the true God? Whose interpretation of *The Bible* should I follow? Why should I believe you, or him, or her, or Joseph Smith, or the Apostle, Paul, or Jim Jones, or Billy Graham, or Oral Roberts, or Mary Baker Eddy, or the Pope, or anyone else on this subject? What test is an appropriate and reliable test to apply to the claims of such as these? Does morality even require a God? Are these not fair questions? Wouldn't a just God expect me to ask such questions?

In the 2001 movie, "Kapax" (Screenplay by Charles Leavitt, based on the novel by Gene Brewer), Prot, who professes to be an alien from the planet Kapax (played by Kevin Spacey) is asked by a psychiatrist, Dr. Mark Powell (played by Jeff Bridges) how K-Paxians know right from wrong in the absence of courts and laws. "Every being in the universe knows right from wrong, Mark" responds, Prot. In the Mormon theology a similar belief is held.

Mormons believe that "the Spirit of Christ is given to every man, that he may know good from evil." (*Book of Mormon, The Book of Moroni.* Compare to page 522 of the 1981 edition.) This, Mormon's believe, is the conscience of man that is in each of us. It is understood to be the inherent spiritual awareness of the difference between right and wrong that we are born with. It is taught and understood to be a feeling of recognition for truth that transcends the cognitive awareness associated with intellectual processing of information. I think that the known physical realities of the universe are such that it makes sense that something other than cognitive awareness is found within us that can experience some sense of harmony with truth, under certain circumstances. There is no question that the entire universe is made up of matter and energy, including us. This matter and energy remains in motion, to a certain degree. At least some of the subatomic particles that are, at once, part of us are somewhat transient in their ability and propensity to pass from us, to and through the world of our immediate surroundings, and then, potentially, back to us. This movement involves energy. We share energy with our surroundings. This energy moves within the realm of and in a manner that is consistent with the dominant electro-magnetic forces that exist at the subatomic level of the matter that makes up the world in which we live. Accordingly, a certain cosmic harmony, or at times potential discord, exists in the world that includes us with or without our cognitive perception of it. I believe that it is not unreasonable or superstitious, but unquestionably the case, that this cosmic harmony or discord is detected by our sensory perceptions on some level, without cognitive processing. In this way, I am convinced that we not only can, but do, feel harmony, or discord, in the universe, on some level. This harmony or discord involves energy. We feel the energy of our universe. Within the Mormon and other religious cultures, this energy can be colloquially referred to as "light" or "spirit". Why not? Such is not far from the truth. These are terms of agreed convention. In a world of cultural and intellectual diversity the conventions governing the use and application of terminology can vary. With this more open attitude about terminology, it seems easy to accept the existence of a form of tightly defined spirituality as part of our universe. It depends on what one means by "spirituality". Frankly, I think the rejection of such involves as much dogmatism and intellectual bias, by those who feel it necessary in the maintenance of their atheism to reject spirituality than is typically attributed to the religious. Of course, I should acknowledge that atheism does not necessarily reject all forms of spirituality, as here described. I think, however, that it does reject that spirituality associated with the supernatural, as well, I believe, it should.

Even though there may be some merit to the theoretical concept of the physical reality of the harmony of truth, I believe this reality about the human condition exists apart from and does not require or depend on a belief in the divine authority of the Church of Jesus Christ of Latter Day Saints as sole possessors of the exclusive agency of God on earth, neither does it depend on the existence of a God as specifically and uniquely defined by the Mormons. The Mormon priesthood leadership is, before and after anything else, a group of fallible men who are understandably anxious about the power and influence that they are able to assert in the lives of their membership. Is the true and larger objective of this influence the maintenance and perpetuation of its own power and continuity; or simply the enlightenment of its constituent members on behalf of a God whose primary concern is not the continuity of His agents, but rather the exaltation of His individual children? This is not a question that is encouraged by proselytizing missionaries of the Mormon Church. It is not a trivial or insignificant question. It is a profoundly relevant question. One that any God, who truly is God, must surely expect and want His spirit children to attend to with a great deal of diligence, concern, and careful scrutiny before accepting anyone as His only uniquely authorized agents on earth, who will impose upon members of His church enormous taxes on their time, talents, and incomes, in exchange for passage into the Celestial Kingdom in the next life and the right to be in attendance to see their children married in the Mormon temple in this life.

Ironically, the Church's own scripture warns of the fallibilities of corruption by authority. In the Church's own *Doctrine and Covenants*, we find:

> We have learned by sad experience that it is the nature and disposition of almost all men, as soon as they get a little authority, as they suppose, they will immediately begin to exercise unrighteous dominion. Hence many are called, but few are chosen. (*Doctrine & Covenants, Section 121.* Compare to page 242 of the 1981 edition.)

Religious authority, as it turns out, is perhaps, among the easiest paths to dominion over the hearts and minds of large groups of people. Quite understandably, most of us are conditioned from infancy to yearn for the simple security of an authority figure from whom a sense of peace and comfort follows from our trust and obedience. As we grow older, a relatively seamless transition occurs as our caregivers, the catalysts we look to for the fulfillment of our anticipated desires, gently transplant our faith in them to other religious authorities to whom we are taught to look for direction, comfort, and security. We are quickly taught that our absentee benefactor, a benevolent God, has appointed agents of His power and authority through whom we learn of His will concerning us. This will, of course, includes obedience to our parents and obedience to religious authorities, as it is administered to us through them.

This social pattern is as old as recorded history. Whether it originated in truth or in deception, there is no question that it has been repeatedly usurped and corrupted throughout the ages for the express purpose of accomplishing the domination and exploitation of the productive output of entire kingdoms and cultures throughout generations of time.

Ironically, the Mormon theology and the philosophy of the famous atheist and author of the philosophy of Objectivism, Ayn Rand, appears to have somewhat of a fleetingly superficial consistency on one point. The *Book of Mormon* Prophet, Nephi, declares, "Adam fell that men might be; and men are that they might have joy." (*Book of Mormon, The Second Book of Nephi.* Compare to page 59 of the 1981 edition.) Ayn Rand declares, "The Objectivist ethics holds man's life as the standard of value – and his own life as the ethical purpose of every individual man." Ayn Rand further explains, "Man must choose his actions, values and goals by the standard of that which is proper to man – in order to achieve, maintain, fulfill and enjoy that ultimate value, that end in itself, which is his own life." (*The Virtue of Selfishness,* p. 25.) Each of the two philosophical arguments suggests some measure of developmental self-actualization as the purpose or meaning of man's existence. However, the two philosophies immediately and irreconcilably part ways. The essence of Mormon theology teaches that joy, for man, is best found in loosing himself in the self sacrificing service of others, as directed by the Mormon priesthood. Ayn Rand, on the other hand, holds that no external agency can or ought to determine for man his course or purpose, but rather that, "Man must choose his actions, values and goals by the standard of that which is proper to man". Ayn Rand argues that life must be pursued in "rational selfishness" and maintains that "the rational interests of men do not clash". She argues that "there is no conflict of interests among men who do not desire the unearned, who do not make sacrifices nor accept them, who deal with one another as traders, giving value for value." (*The Virtue of Selfishness*, p. 31.)

It is a poignant paradox that the Mormon culture is programmed to treat with derisive disrespect the suggestion that the claims of authority on behalf of God made by the Mormon leadership should be considered with utmost diligence to the intellectual discipline of strict objective scrutiny of all relevant facts, questions, and inconsistencies. Such an approach is deemed to bear the influence of Satan. Alternatively, abdication of the God-given intellectual faculties involved in objective scrutiny is required, while an emotional based belief in apparently implausible and fantastic claims is encouraged with the warmth of social acceptance into a community anxious to be strengthened by another convert. The new convert's time and talents are needed to sustain what may well be unsustainable without feeding the Church's voracious appetite for the sacrifices of new members to continue its world-wide and increasingly political objectives. Ayn Rand's Objectivism, on the other hand, holds that "rationality is man's basic virtue". By Ayn Rand's definition, it would appear that rationality "means the recognition and acceptance of reason as one's only guide to action". She argues that navigation of the course of one's life should involve "one's total commitment to a state of full, conscious awareness, to the maintenance of a full mental focus in all issues, in all choices, in all of one's waking hours" and that we should be dedicated to "the fullest perception of reality within one's power and to the constant, active expansion of one's perception..." (*The Virtue of Selfishness*, p. 31.)

Oddly, it would seem that the atheist, Ayn Rand's, prescription for navigating life is more consistent with the Godly objective of intellectual development and personal responsibility, while the Mormon philosophy advocates the abdication of the reasoning process in a rush to accept the opportunity to subordinate one's life to the interpretations of God's will and the sacrifices required of us by others. I suggest to my readers that you have not really studied your own religion or any religion until you have carefully considered the observations of Ayn Rand in *The Virtue of Selfishness* as a counterpoint that warrants attention.

The Mormon Church has a deeply vested financial interest in promoting its own short cut to epistemological and intellectual discipline in quick acceptance of its authority as God's exclusive agents on earth. By reasonable estimates, that interest is ten percent of all your future earnings and twenty to eighty percent of all your available discretionary time, devoted to service in the ever growing Church. More often than not, this sacrifice comes at the expense of your own personal and family needs and relationships. Ayn Rand, on the other hand, simply loved the consistency of truth as discovered through the reasoning process, and enjoyed sharing the merits of scrutiny as a key element of a happy, ethical, responsible, and successful life.

One need not feel limited to a choice between Mormonism and atheism, a la Ayn Rand, to recognize the relevance of the divergent philosophies to one's own thoughtful consideration of the very real and relevant question about what level and measure of scrutiny might be appropriate to apply to the prospect of yielding one's life in deference to the professed priesthood authority of another.

Chapter 6

Challenges to Scrutiny

A variety of factors commonly contribute to a strong feeling of emotional resistance, or a mental block, in many, if not most of society, to the process of intellectual scrutiny of one's own religious beliefs. Generally, for a variety of reasons discussed in previous chapters, we want to believe what we want to believe so strongly that this desire transmutes itself into an equally powerful desire to repress our own awareness of actual and real evidences that might pose a challenge to our chosen belief. While most of us will want to be counted among those who are aware that this emotional trap is commonly found in human behavior, very few will have the courage to allow for the realization that their own religious beliefs may be infected with this intellectual sickness, let alone allow such an awareness to rise to the level of conscious cognitive consideration. Fewer still, will actually see and acknowledge that this is the case, even when it is obviously so. There are a variety of reasons for this, not the least of which being the intense desire and emotional need to conform our philosophical and religious beliefs to the social demands of the clique of our choice in order to get along comfortably. Often, our very economic survival requires this conformity of us. In past cultures and some present cultures people's very lives depend on religious conformity. In the western world, we like to think that we are above religious discrimination. In actuality, from the moment the Puritans landed in the New World, our hypocrisy in this area has been made manifest and continues. Fortunately, the competing hypocrisies of our political system, one party always anxious to point out the injustices and fallibilities of the other, continues to contribute to a judiciary that supports prosecution of those who would engage in the indiscriminant slaughter of independent and free thinking individuals. Such was not always the case in the New World. Please forgive that flippant and cheeky observation. I share it with you because I don't think it is entirely devoid of some merit as a sardonic commentary on our system, even though I realize that our founding fathers who crafted the Declaration of Independence and the Constitution should be given the credit they deserve, along with thoughtful judges who attempt to reconcile their decisions with constitutional principles. Some, even Mormons, would argue that the integrity of the judiciary is disintegrating at the lower levels and increasingly caving in to the very political and social pressures that it was established to keep in check. I truly wonder how long we would be able to expect the judiciary to maintain the semblance of objectivity in support of constitutional principles in a society where any religious majority accomplished dominating political influence. The judiciary is, after all, appointed. Regression to the indiscriminant slaughter of independent and free thinking individuals is not likely to occur in my life time. However, one of the dirty little secrets that we don't like to talk about, is the fact that the judiciary is overwhelmed and law enforcement has been given potentially dangerous liberty with the "prosecutorial discretion" to be selective in the application of judicial resources, in order to ease the burden on the system. I don't recommend childish naivety in contemplating how that plays out in communities dominated by a particular religious majority. I'm not suggesting here that murder of religious dissenters is commonly overlooked by prosecutors, but rather, that where politically influenced discretion is applied, to pick and choose where to apply the limited resources of prosecuting justice, the complaints of the most politically significant constituents will enjoy an unfair share of the attention of prosecuting and law enforcement resources, while the unpopular constituents will find themselves left quite vulnerable to the ramifications of not enough judicial and law enforcement resources to go around. Let's also consider that city councils, school boards, and local government agencies generally reflect the social and philosophical (religious) demographics of the local communities they serve, as do chambers of commerce and economic development agencies. Some find it unnerving that the Utah Republican Party offices are found in a building across the street from the Mormon Church's executive offices in Salt Lake City. Even more unnerving to some, is the fact that in the basement of the building housing the Utah Republican Party offices are also found tunnels with direct access, not only to the Mormon Church's executive offices, but also the President of the Church's private condominium in an adjacent complex.

Mormon communities, whether or not they constitute the political majority in the cities and townships in which they are found, are still very tight-knit communities that look out for their own in a variety of ways. To be an active Mormon is to have economic encouragement, support, and opportunities within the Mormon community. To be seen to question the principles of Mormonism is to be perceived to be "unworthy" of economic success in the minds of many members of the church. A corresponding self-fulfilling prophecy can be accomplished in some communities, and often is. To question is to risk a lot. Social and economic isolation as a result of very real, yet plausibly deniable, religious discrimination is not at all out of the question. I am aware from personal experience and from the anecdotal observations of others, who I trust, that in some communities, where Mormons see themselves as having achieved political "critical mass", plausible deniability amidst overt religious discrimination isn't even given a second thought. A sense of impunity, in some communities, rises to the level of being scary.

Let Mormon apologists say what they may in response to this claim. The matter is easily tested. Try publishing a detailed commentary about philosophical weaknesses in the Mormon theology under your own name on the internet so that it can be easily found when your name is "googled". Then spend the next year applying for jobs and/or rental units in certain counties in Utah and Idaho. Good luck to you. Many Mormons in Utah will not even allow their children to play with "non-Mormons". A good friend of mine, who no longer believes in the faith, has decided to wait till her son graduates from high school before asking to have her name removed from the records of the Church, in order to spare her son the social isolation and discrimination that she is convinced, on the basis of her first hand experience, will surely follow. For these, and other more general social reasons that have nothing in particular to do with Mormonism, a tendency to subordinate one's philosophical and/or religious choices to group pressure is common. Thoughtful consideration of the merits of one's own philosophical underpinnings is quite rare notwithstanding the fact that one's philosophy defines one's life and who one is.

The French aristocrat, Alexis de Tocqueville, spotted the suffocation of American intellectual independence in the 1830's, and commented on its demise in his work *Democracy in America*.

> In that immense crowd which throngs the avenues to power in the United States, I found very few men who displayed that manly candor and masculine independence of opinion which frequently distinguished the Americans in former times, and which constitutes the leading feature in distinguished characters wheresoever they may be found. (Alexis de Tocqueville, *Democracy in America*, 1835.

Compare to page 120 of the 1984 edition of Richard D. Heffner's abridgement.)

De Tocqueville explains the American social dynamic that gives rise to this suffocation.

> In America the majority raises formidable barriers around the liberty of opinion. Within these barriers, an author may write what he pleases, but woe to him if he goes beyond them. Not that he is in danger of an auto-da-fe', but he is exposed to continued obloquy and persecution. Before publishing his opinions he imagined that he held them in common with others; but no sooner has he declared them, than he is loudly censured by his opponents, whilst those who think like him, without having the courage to speak out, abandon him in silence.

De Tocqueville warns of the dangers for those who dare to violate the constraints of political correctness, as follows:

> Fetters and headsman were the course instruments which tyranny formerly employed; but the civilization of our ages has perfected despotism itself... Monarchs had, so to speak, materialized oppression. The democratic republics of the present day have rendered it as entirely an affair of the mind, as the will which it is intended to coerce. Under the absolute sway of one man, the body was attacked in order to subdue the soul; but the soul escaped the blows which were directed against it, and rose proudly superior. Such is not the course adopted by tyranny in democratic republics. There the body is left free, and the soul is enslaved. The master no longer says, "You shall think as I do or you shall die". Rather, he says, "You are free to think differently from me, and to retain your life, your property, and all that you possess, but you are henceforth a stranger among your people. You may retain your civil rights, but they will be useless to you, for you will never be chosen by your fellow-citizens, if you solicit their votes; and they will affect to scorn you, if you ask for their esteem. You will remain among men, but you will be de-

prived of the rights of mankind. Your fellow-creatures
will shun you like an impure being; and even those who
believe in your innocence will abandon you, lest they
should be shunned in their turn. Go in peace! I have given
you your life, but it is an existence worse than death.
(Alexis de Tocqueville, *Democracy in America,* 1835.
Compare to pages 117-118 of the 1984 edition of Richard
D. Heffner's abridgement.)

Opinions will vary, as to whether de Tocqueville's
observations about the tyranny of the majority, or what we
now refer to as "political correctness", are a fair assessment
of the American democratic social dynamic. Similarly,
opinions will vary, as to the extent that this dynamic may be
seen in the Mormon sub-culture. My opinion is this: Alex de
Tocqueville was an insightful genius. For my progeny, your
education is incomplete until you study his work thoroughly.
For civic leaders, your preparation for public service is
wanting until you familiarize yourself with Alexis de
Tocqueville's insightful observations. He "nailed", with
surgical precision, the problem that the social demands for
"political correctness" would become, and the tyranny with
which the opinions of the majority would shout down and
obliterate respectful consideration of honest and sincere
dissention. Certain elements of the American religious right
have become an oppressive force that seeks neither justice,
nor equity, nor thoughtfulness, but rather perpetuation of its
own power to politically and socially suffocate what it fears
most. In fairness, we should acknowledge that certain
elements of the non-religious left share similar goals. I dare
say that the clearest example of this social dynamic that I
have seen is experienced in Mormon congregations. God
help you if you express a thoughtful observation about the
implausibility of a canonized doctrinal principle or question
the ethics of the priesthood leadership. You will be left with
your skin... barely. You will look down and check it to see if
it is still there and if you still exist, because your welcome
will rapidly and ever so quietly evaporate. You will wonder

if you are still in the room, because your presence will no longer be acknowledged if it can be avoided. So it is that to question is to risk what most are afraid to risk. Hence, the suspension of the rational processes of the mind, in an effort to avoid cognitive awareness of obvious questions, becomes a requirement of social survival in the Mormon culture.

The external threat of different forms and levels of isolation, to gently coerce at least the appearance of philosophical conformity, is actually quite common in most societies and cultures. A couple of specific psychological barriers to scrutiny, or intellectual independence, permeate every aspect of the Mormon culture. They are, on their own merits, powerful deterrents and contribute to the risks of isolation. These devices employ the member's own ego in a couple of different ways. The first of these devices to immerge, in the life of the Mormon, is the public "bearing of testimony", which reinforces the attachment of the member's own openly declared beliefs with their public persona. Now their credibility needs to be maintained to preserve a social standing that is enmeshed with the listeners' acceptance and approval, not only of the individual, but of the individual on the basis of the relative merits and apparent strength and foundation of their professed belief. Children of Mormon families are encouraged, from a very young age, to openly and regularly share, not only their belief that the church is true, but their perceived basis for those beliefs. These declarations are referred to as "bearing testimony". The importance of "bearing testimony", to a Mormon, is significant. In a particular verse, in the *Doctrine and Covenants,* the Lord is reported to have declared to various Elders of the Church that their testimonies were "recorded in heaven for the angels to look upon; and they rejoice over you, and your sins are forgiven you..." (*Doctrine & Covenants, Section 62.* Compare to page 114 of the 1981 edition.) It is a common belief among Mormons, often encouraged by their priesthood leaders, that the "bearing of testimony" not only brings souls to the fold, but has the added advantage of contributing to the absolution of the sins of the testifier. With this considerable motivation, members are encouraged to share their testimonies often, and regular monthly congregational meetings are dedicated for this purpose. Obviously, it is the hope and belief that the listeners will be touched by the testimony, and "feel" impressed to share the belief. Not so obvious, but even more significant, is the impact of this process on the person doing the testifying. Rare is the individual who, once taking a public position on an important philosophical or religious subject, will feel comfortable with publicly reversing that position. It's a credibility thing. Mormons are encouraged to share their testimonies as often as possible, and generally the active and devout ones do. This reinforces their personal belief and the psychological mental block that emerges as an obstacle to reconsider and publicly reverse that belief. Now, reconsidering our belief not only requires the emotional leap over the substantial personal hurdle of what we may wish to be true, but also, at this point, the social hurdle of loosing face with our peers. For this reason, even the millions of Mormons who become disenchanted with the Church, or fall into inactivity for a variety of reasons, rarely openly disavow their previous testimonies. More often than not, they simply slip quietly into a state of inactivity. I'm sure my family wishes that I could have just left my philosophical shift at that.

We have a tendency, in our society, to view open corrections of previously stated beliefs to be evidence of foolishness. This is understandable, but I think unfortunate. If we are not evolving human beings, growing in knowledge, and wisdom, and enlightenment, that is an unfortunate thing. To impose upon ourselves social barriers to reconsideration of the foundation of our beliefs and paradigms, when appropriate, is to limit ourselves to a self-imposed intellectual damnation for the dubious payoff of maintaining the stability of relationships based on self-limiting pressures. Are such relationships really worth preserving at that price?

Moving on through the life of an active member of the Mormon Church, a significant series of challenges to the member's openness to objective scrutiny of their own beliefs emerges, as the member is "co-opted" into the Church's system of leadership development. For those unfamiliar with the term, "co-opt" is defined as, among other things, "To neutralize or win over (an independent minority, for example) through assimilation into an established group or culture: *co-opt rebels by giving them a position of authority.*" *(thefreedictionary.com.)* Co-opting, as a political technique, is as old as civilization, perhaps older. Typically, men's resistance to authority, on all levels, is easily bought off with participation in that authority. In the more overt and obvious examples of the "co-opt", men's open resistance to the assertion of authority is "bought off" with appointments to subordinate positions of power and authority, bringing economic rewards as part of that authority. Allegiance is purchased with participation in the spoils of dominating control. In its more subtle forms, the "co-opt" can be accomplished even more effectively, at a far cheaper price, and often is. In the Mormon experience, the attention of individuals, already anxious to believe that God's authority is vested in the Church for a variety of reasons, is easily distracted from the process of thorough and objective scrutiny of the legitimacy of the Church's claims, as they are informed that they have been chosen by God to be a part of the Church's leadership and need to immediately begin training in preparation for their new callings. The prospect of the increased social standing, respect, deference, and endorsements from higher authorities is hard to resist for most men. Mormon men, whose marriages may be struggling, often find dramatic shifts in the dynamic of their relationships upon being called to significant positions of leadership in the Church. Devout Mormon wives often find it easier to overlook imperfections of their husbands, that previously seemed intolerable, when they learn that God, apparently, thinks he's worthy of a position of significant leadership in the Church. Maybe, she thinks, she was being too hard on him. It's a bit more challenging to maintain the support of her Mormon "sisters in the faith", in discussions of his inadequacies, while his worthiness and leadership qualifications are being extolled from the pulpit by higher authorities, calling upon the local congregation to support and pray for their new leader. It's difficult for an average man to question the legitimacy of the authority of God's agents when those agents are informing him that God has chosen him to receive the honors of leadership in His church. Clearly, these men must be inspired. In this way, the ecclesiastical order of the Mormon Church, made up largely of a part time, volunteer, clergy is integral to the success of the Church and contributes greatly to the psychological glue that holds it together, year after year, and generation after generation. Through the opportunities for leadership, made generally available to all male members of the Mormon Church, no matter what their other accomplishments in life may be, both those who are successful in their careers, as well as the relatively unfulfilled, have an equal opportunity in the Church to experience the ego boost of Church leadership. This leadership comes with the enormous deference from members that it entails and the regular personal endorsements from higher leaders that are routinely part of the discipline of Mormon leadership. It would be unfair to suggest that most of those who serve in Church leadership positions have sought for this ego boost as the primary motivation for their advancement in the priesthood. Few are likely to admit that this is their motivation for Church devotion. In my personal experience in the Mormon priesthood, I think many, if not most, have a far more humble and philosophical attitude about their service. Generally, the average Mormon, in my experience, sincerely believes in the doctrine of the Church and the Plan of

Salvation and willingly contributes generously of his time and talents to the Church for that reason, taking whatever priesthood assignments come in stride. There is no question however, humans being who and what they are, that years of Church leadership service reinforce a paradigm of belief that is inhospitable to fundamental questions that run across the social grain of a life built around relationships invested in those same beliefs and a social order that personally validates the individual in question.

Aside from the challenges to objective scrutiny of one's own beliefs discussed above, the simple matter of objective intellectual discipline remains to be considered. Objectivity, I think, is becoming a lost art in America. I remember, in grade school, a teacher of mine spent considerable time impressing upon our young minds the discipline of critical, objective thinking. I wish I could remember her name. She deserves an honorable mention. Each week, a certain time would be dedicated to sharing current events clipped from a newspaper. The students who wanted to participate brought clipped news articles and shared briefly what they were about and what they thought about them. That insightful teacher would not leave it at that. Even at our young ages, she worked with us to identify unsupported premises in articles, and explained to us the intellectual discipline of objectivity. Somehow she used a vocabulary that we could understand to help us grasp the point that far more consideration was regularly required to get to the truth of a matter than simply accepting someone else's report at face value. She helped us become aware that falsehood could easily be passed off as truth, to the naïve, by someone who has a personal agenda and a little skill with spin. I have never since seen or heard of a teacher who engaged her students with such dedication to such an important lesson of life and such an important and relevant lesson about learning. Unfortunately, we now hear more often of teachers smuggling their own politics and religious and social beliefs into their lesson plans while discouraging objectivity. The immergence of this same philosophical corruption in our judiciary is evidenced, too frequently, by publicly aired reality "court" type programs in which judges routinely impose upon litigants their own moral and social lectures reflecting clear biases that are peripheral to the legal issues before them. I have watched, in dismay, as these lectures reflect the impunity of judges who display no reflective sensitivity, whatsoever, that their behavior is being aired on network television, obviously confident in the general absence of any risk of a backlash from viewers who still recognize the fundamental constitutional principles they are trampling on.

Surely, in this vast country, there are a few who still teach the principles of critical thinking and objective analysis. I don't think, however, that their peers would necessarily be jumping at the chance to call attention to their attentiveness to the subject matter. This is not something that is celebrated in our society. Rather, in my experience, it is feared. Generally, those who are most skilled with and sensitive to the principles and mechanics of objectivity are intimidating to those who aren't. Our world, politics what they are, generally sustains itself on the basis of a preponderance of "BS". People's willingness and ease with accepting and overlooking "BS" is of higher value, in most organizational structures, than those who challenge it. Middle management, often being quite full of "BS", does not look favorably on those who recognize it. Insightful and independent thinking people are not generally singled out or recommended for promotion. In short, objectivity is not encouraged enough in American culture. "Political correctness" is encouraged too much. As a result, the skill and discipline of objectivity is becoming increasingly rare, along with the willingness to apply it openly, by those who still possess it. This is a cultural travesty that, in my own opinion, impacts on our culture and manifests itself in the form of the economic struggles we face. The discipline of intellectual objectivity is the discipline of fairness, and justice, and good sense. It is not the particular high point of the average politician's character composition. Consequently, it is not the particular high point of the character composition of our national or state legislatures. Neither is it, for example, the discipline with which mortgage banking executives, with incentive compensation packages based on mortgage loan origination volumes, were permitted to get away with the ridiculous and indiscriminant liberalization of mortgage loan qualifying criteria. They would be paid millions in volume based compensation, while being fully aware that this policy would contribute to a real estate bubble that would burst, wreaking havoc on the American economy. They would be cashed out with their bonuses before the problem manifested itself, then, potentially, paid additional bonuses from the government bailout proceeds. It seems fair to surmise that discussions about the reasonableness of the policies that gave rise to this opportunity did not exemplify a great deal of thoughtful objective discipline. I'm sure personal motivations impacted on the policy presentations, and some mix between intellectual laziness and outright self-interest resulted in policy approvals that would have been found to have no rational support in an intellectually disciplined environment.

Thoughtful, disciplined, intellectual objectivity takes a certain awareness of one's own intellectual fallibility and, accordingly, employs a willingness to continually keep it in check by painstakingly applying rigorous efforts to check and double check one's own conclusions with a variety of cross validating tests before accepting something to be true. This rigorous discipline is particularly challenging in our culture, from my experience, because it is generally perceived to be obnoxious by some and mean spirited and demeaning by others. I have lost track of the number of times I have found legitimate observations about the fatal logical flaws in a proposed course or policy to be met with personal insults directed at the critic and his motivations. I'm sure we've all experienced this in life. As a Mormon, I, personally, have been subjected to this type of condemnation by leaders of the Mormon Church, and members of my own family, in the face of entirely legitimate and well founded observations about the conduct of the Mormon priesthood.

Chapter 7

Ostensible Truth

The simple reality is that there is no, known, objectively verifiable, evidence that conclusively supports the larger claims of Mormonism, like general Christianity, or any other religion that I am aware of. Volumes are written with presentations of peripheral "evidences" that seemingly corroborate the Mormon faith, in general, with discussions of eye witness accounts of miracles, archeological findings that seem supportive of the ancient American cultures of the *Book of Mormon;* apparent Biblical consistencies with certain doctrinal positions on baptism, Sabbath day worship, tithing, priesthood hierarchy and succession of authority, and a variety of other positions and claims of the Church. None of this evidence conclusively supports the claims of the Mormon Church to the elimination of all reasonable doubt or skepticism on the merits of the evidence itself. In the case of Mormonism, the absence of objectively verifiable evidence is actually incorporated into the doctrine of the Church, which argues openly that it is an essential part of God's plan that we must rely on the promptings of the Holy Ghost, confirming, with feelings, the veracity of another's testimony to us, to properly acquire a spiritually based testimony of the Church. Were this not essential to God's plan, as presented by the Mormon's, God might have done a variety of things to make the investigation of the claims of the church a far simpler process. For instance, the "golden plates", from which Joseph Smith translated the *Book of Mormon,* might not have been conveniently returned to the angel, Moroni, for safekeeping and beyond the reach of scrutiny. The Bible might have been written a little less ambiguously in areas that seem to be open to a wide range of subjective interpretation in order to arrive at the interpretive conclusions the Mormon's require to support their faith. The financial rewards that are routinely promised to follow the enormous contributions in money and time that the Church requires for temple worthiness might be a little more consistent without the need to invoke the, "Well, sometimes God needs to test your faith", explanation, when you find yourself making choices between paying the rent or tithing.

The Mormon Church makes no pretense of offering objectively verifiable evidence of the veracity of its claim of unique authority as God's exclusive agents on earth. Rather, it sends its missionaries out to share the good news of its divine role on earth to whoever may hear the message. By accepting the message to be true, candidates demonstrate their worthiness for God's continuing grace and blessings in their lives. Those who hear the message and reject it in this life are deemed to be unworthy of eternal progress and consigned to a form of spiritual damnation in the eternities. As a practical matter, the missionaries of the Church must offer something a little more substantial than "it's us" as a catalyst for conversion, and so a variety of doctrinal lessons are offered with their scriptural "evidences" for the investigator's consideration. The essence of these lessons differs significantly from the message of the average protestant evangelist. Clearly, the Mormon message must, necessarily, turn the attention of the prospect, quickly, from "follow Jesus"; to "follow us, as Jesus' exclusive agents on earth, uniquely authorized to receive direction from Him, in these 'latter days' for the benefit of the entire world". Otherwise, the case for being the exclusive custodians for Jesus' tithing receipts, which in the Mormon protocol are mandatory for exaltation in His kingdom, would become moot. No general worthiness credit is granted for charitable contributions of time or money made to other worthy causes or organizations. Only donations made directly to the Church of Jesus Christ of Latter Day Saints, for which a receipt is issued by the Church, qualify the candidate for temple worthiness, and, therefore, exaltation in God's Kingdom. As God's exclusive agents on earth, the determination of worthiness of charitable causes for financial backing is the sole province of the Mormon priesthood leadership. This agency is strictly applied. Even charitable causes recommended to the members for contributions, for which the Mormon Church makes its collections system available, are generally excluded as qualifying contributions for tithing and temple worthiness purposes. So, when the Mormon leaders, for instance, recommend that their members make liberal individual contributions to benefit Haitian earthquake victims through the Mormon collection system, members understand that, if they wish to continue to be considered worthy of a temple recommend, they must only contribute to the earthquake victims what they can afford to contribute after already making their tithing contributions to the Church. There is nothing cheap about being a "worthy" Mormon. Make no mistake it is a very, very expensive proposition. Something, then, must be offered to prospective members as a fairly compelling basis for a spiritual manifestation that the Church's claim of being the exclusive agency of God is true. It isn't going to be objectively verifiable, nor is it going to be conclusive, so it needs to be fairly compelling on a social and emotional level and it needs to seem fairly convincing in a well guided cursory review of historical details and Biblical passages. More importantly, the body of active members needs to be very well trained and very motivated to receive new prospective members into the fold with welcoming arms and social warmth and reassurance. The bottom line is that the new prospect's emerging faith will be largely based on "spiritual" feelings. The more welcoming the existing members are to the new prospects, the more likely those "spiritual" feelings of validation will be.

I dare say that there is no organization on the face of the earth that dedicates more relative time and resources to the training and motivation of its membership to receive and embrace new prospective members. Rising to the call of missionary service, for devout Mormons, is a solemn obligation weighing in heavily on the scale of worthiness for eternal rewards. It is a matter of considerable classroom attention, doctrinal dedication, family devotion, specialized leadership attention, publishing resource allocation, statistical reporting and review, and priesthood performance evaluation. Placement of the *Book of Mormon* with investigators, investigators visiting in church, doctrinal discussions with investigators, invitations made, family follow-ups with investigators, missionary "referrals" to investigators, and, ultimately, convert baptisms, are tracked, reported and monitored carefully. Goal setting sessions are held regularly, and review and reporting on accomplishments toward those goals is a constant ongoing part of the management of the Mormon Church. Virtually every Mormon sponsored activity is expected to have one or more "priesthood purposes" and at least one of those "priesthood purposes" is expected to be an outreach effort of some sort. The Mormon leadership, having risen through the ranks of the Mormon Church on the basis of the combination of their Church devotion and vocational success, which affords them the time to increasingly devote to the Church, are comprised of very successful men in their own right, who know how to motivate and manage the minds and hearts of their Mormon followers. With worthiness for exaltation always on the line, and continued social acceptance at even greater risk, Mormons remain devoted to an astounding degree, often far beyond their reasonable emotional capacities. Mormon women fall into clinical depression under the pressure to keep up the pace of the social demands in greater numbers, by some reports, than their general Christian counterparts. Mormonism can be exhausting for some. Generally speaking, devout members of the Mormon Church are not unaware of the enormous sacrifices required of them. They take a sense of personal satisfaction, with considerable social validation, that their faith measures up to the challenges. Devout Mormons believe that their personal sacrifices in this life will be rewarded, in the life to come, with eternal rewards. Meanwhile, the Mormon Church expands its holdings and encourages the personal sacrifices of its devoted members, in the name of God.

I'm sure I could dedicate a few hundred pages of discussion to most of the more salient doctrinal positions of the Church and the relative merits and flaws of the arguments in their defense, in an effort to bring the reader up to speed with the ostensible evidences of the truth of the Church's professed authority. I don't really see the point. Exhaustive works can be found on detailed doctrinal positions. Perhaps, one day I'll add my own. However, the fact remains that not even the Mormon Church considers any of this evidence to be conclusive, but rather a suggestive basis for asking God in prayer for a confirmation of the truth of the matter of the Church's authority. Confirmation is supposed to come from the Holy Ghost, in the form of feelings. Devout Mormons will argue that these feelings are spiritual and have nothing to do with the social influence the prospective members find themselves surrounded with. I was convinced of that myself, for most of my adult life. I had what I believed to be a deep, spiritual, testimony that the Mormon Church was true. I was convinced that the scriptures supported the Church's position on a wide array of topics. I read the *Book of Mormon* several times and felt an increasing conviction that it truly was an ancient historical record brought forth by the power of God. I was moved by stories of the Prophet, Joseph Smith, and his "martyrdom". I learned to be a devoted and dutiful priesthood member, always anxious to serve, and grow, and accept more priesthood responsibilities and assignments. I was married in the temple and I tried my best to live by the teachings of the Church for as long as I believed. In short, I was sincere. Not perfect, by any stretch of the imagination, but very sincere.

Sincerity is an interesting thing. I think sincerity has very much to do with the conviction and devotion of most members of the Mormon Church in more ways than the obvious. Most Mormons, in my experience, are sincere about their faith, for the most part. That is not to say that they don't exhibit their occasional human weaknesses and hypocrisies. We all do. Generally, in my experience, I think Mormons are found to be quite sincere, as a general rule. Sincerity is a powerful thing. Sincerity brings with it a certain spirit or feeling. The innocence of a child is charming and heartwarming. It makes us feel good. We all remember being children. We remember believing what mom told us. We remember wanting to believe. We remember the comfort that our little cocoons of belief provided for us. We remember trying to be good because mom told us we should. We remember the good feeling that came over us when we were good and particularly when it was recognized. Many of us remember the experiences of extending kindnesses as children to others and having kindnesses extended to us. We remember feeling safe and associating those feelings of safety with goodness and kindness. We remember that adults related to us differently then, than they do now. Most adults went out of their way to be gentle, sensitive, supportive, and fair. The spirit of that kind of human dynamic feels good. It feels safe. It feels profoundly comfortable. It is heartwarming. Mormons generally, in my experience, love those types of feelings and love perpetuating an environment in which those types of feelings are fostered and nurtured. They are, for the most part, sincere people who are thoughtful, to a point. Unfortunately, due to cultural pressure, that point, all too often, stops short of critical objective analysis in the face of potential controversy. A contributing factor is the weight of the Mormon cultural value placed on the absence of "contention", which is deemed to be "of Satan". In the

Doctrine and Covenants, a particular passage has the Lord explaining that the "true points of doctrine" were brought to light to avoid contention. "And this I do that I may establish my gospel, that there may not be so much contention; yea, Satan doth stir up the hearts of the people to contention concerning the points of my doctrine; and in these things they do err, for they do wrest the scriptures and do not understand them." (*Doctrine & Covenants, Section 10.* See page 20 of the 1981 edition.) Similarly, the *Book of Mormon* teaches, "For verily, verily I say unto you, he that hath the spirit of contention is not of me, but is of the devil, who is the father of contention, and he stirreth up the hearts of men to contend with anger, one with another." (*Book of Mormon, Third Nephi - The Book of Nephi.* See page 429 of the 1981 edition.)

Mormons are hypersensitive to contention and go to great lengths to avoid it. The culture reinforces the belief that to question the doctrine of the Church or the performance of the priesthood leadership, beyond certain superficial acceptable limits, is to engage in satanic contention and seen as offensive to the Spirit of God. They consider that to "offend" is to be inappropriate and to strive to avoid offending anyone is to strive for perfection. They are particularly sensitive to the New Testament passage in James, which reads, "For in many things we offend all. If any man offend not in word, the same is a perfect man, and able also to bridle the whole body." (*Holy Bible* / King James Version, James 3:2.)

In their quest to cling to the warm and fuzzy feeling of the sweeter moments of their childhood, Mormons go way out of their way to avoid contention. They distance themselves from controversy, when possible, and avoid contributing to it. In this effort, they often overlook what shouldn't be overlooked, in the name of being forgiving or charitable. They discourage discussion of, and often avoid, controversial issues. They satisfy themselves that they are leaving judgment to God, which, in practical terms, in the Mormon culture, boils down to leaving judgment to the local Bishop or higher authorities. By Mormon doctrine, a Bishop is considered, among other things, principally appointed to be "a judge in Israel, to do the business of the church, to sit in judgment upon transgressors upon testimony as it shall be laid before him according to the laws, by the assistance of his counselors, whom he has chosen or will choose among the elders of the church." (*Doctrine & Covenants, Section 107*. See page 220 of the 1981 edition.)

It is the Bishop's unique responsibility to judge members of his congregation on behalf of God and the Church. As this is understood to be the case, Mormons bring many of their marital and family problems to the Bishop for his assessment and counsel. Bishops are called and set apart from amongst High Priests of the Church. In my observation, advancement in the Mormon priesthood is associated closely with an individual's success in adopting and incorporating into their behavioral repertoire a certain gentle, yet confident and authoritative, demeanor that feeds the lay members' need to feel comfortable in the midst of intellectual and emotional surrender of their judgment to higher authorities. It is not unusual to hear comments about how the Church leaders who speak in general church conferences seem to all have a very similar speaking voice and even a certain cadence. They all seem to have gone to the same speech coach. There is no speech coach... there is just the natural tendency for humans to gravitate toward validation and to seize upon that which is seen to work to that end. Mormon's conform to a certain behavior as they travel up the ecclesiastical ladder. This is natural in any organization. It is even more so in the Mormon culture because the doctrine, itself, directs the members toward certain types of behavior for both "spiritual", and more significantly, very practical reasons. When deference to leadership is achieved, priesthood power is achieved. When that deference largely involves the surrender of judgment, ominous power is achieved through willful blindness in the name of spirituality. Unfortunately, this is arguably akin to the kind of corporate cultural blindness found to be at the root of the loss of life in NASA's Columbia mission by the Columbia Accident Investigation Board, who reported that "Organizational barriers at NASA prevent[ed] critical safety communication" (Harold Gehman, *Columbia Accident Investigation Report*, August, 2003) by encouraging an attitude typified by the fear that one's boss might think less of him or her if bothered with concerns amidst the "go fever" that infected the organizational culture. In the Mormon culture there is considerable "go fever" for bringing souls to the fold, and expanding the membership, and therefore tithing revenues of the Church. Ecclesiastical success is measured, in large part, not so much by a congregation's heightened sense of self discovery, self awareness, and self mastery, but rather by the congregation's growth in numbers and "tithing worthiness".

The ostensible truth of the Church, to those who believe, is actually not found simply in the detailed consistency of its doctrines and scriptures, but rather the social and emotional power of the multitudes of testimonies of seemingly credible and sincere people who are often successful in their respective vocations. We like to be associated with success. The unspoken ostensible premise is that successful people who are seemingly credible and sincere don't lie... so they must be telling the truth. Many of these people, it is supposed, "are more accomplished, and more educated, and more spiritual than me, so I can rely on the strength of their testimonies because a warm and confirming spirit seems to confirm to my heart that they are telling the truth". "I want to believe, because they seem like such good people and they advocate good values. I want to be a part of good things. I can look past doubt and unanswered questions. I will believe." It's a choice. Unfortunately, over time, the choice to pursue lofty values and successful relationships can degenerate into a choice to darken one's own intellectual faculties in the face of meaningful questions and an appropriately strict intellectual discipline in handling those questions. It can become a choice and eventually a cultural habit to seek warm and comforting feelings even at the expense of objective discipline. Ultimately, so much of one's life is invested in this culture, with enormous sacrifices, that it becomes too emotionally difficult to consider, for a moment, what is suggested by the increasingly obvious inconsistencies found in the Mormon culture, as it unfolds itself in the life of the member. How something feels becomes, for the devout Mormon, the primary basis for validating truth or identifying the evil spirit of contention. Inevitably, based on the social course of the life of Mormonism, all challenges to doctrine, priesthood legitimacy, and beliefs in general, make the member feel very uncomfortable. This feeling of discomfort is automatically and circularly deemed to be sufficient basis for dismissing the challenge as being of a "dark spirit" and to be avoided. Avoidance behavior becomes an essential characteristic of the Mormon psyche and culture as underscored by the widely employed directive, "don't delve into the mysteries", whenever something challenging and difficult to reconcile emerges in discussions among members. Members are "counseled" to avoid "delving into the mysteries" by trusting in the Church leadership and leaving the difficult and challenging questions to be revealed in God's "own due time". Deeply emotionally and socially invested in the faith of the culture, devout Mormons are only too anxious to have, not only social permission, but even an authoritative directive from God to avoid thoughtful consideration of Church controversies. Inevitably, the Mormon culture is quietly and gently yet profoundly hostile to the essential principles of objectivity. As this is the case, ostensibly good people learn to repress the very clarity of mind that is essential to the maintenance of real social justice. A particular Mormon mom comes to mind. I know her well and have had long conversations with her younger sister, who she deems to be less devout and, therefore, less worthy than herself. Ironically, her sister's observations validate my own in support of the conclusion that some of the patently obvious injustices that she subjects her children and other family members to are egregious in their abuse of the simple principles of fairness. Her relationship with a daughter may already have been irreparably damaged. She has virtually destroyed any realistic hope of a relationship with another family member, on the basis of her own, self righteous and unfounded, condemnations. She seems blind to the reality of her own behavior. Her less active sister seems to see the problem with clarity. She does not. She enjoys the esteem of her Church peers who see her as successful in life and in the Church. Her sister has struggled in her marriage and economically. The younger has a sense of justice and authentic genuine human decency that the older and more devout does not. One clings to the ostensible veracity of the Church for emotional and social support. The other has fleeting doubts, while wanting to believe, but still looks to simple human decency and consistently reconcilable principles of objectivity to measure her authenticity and plot her course. Where there is a bit of doubt and skepticism, in my experience, there is the hope of intellectual humility that liberates the soul. Where there is arrogant confidence of spirit that suffocates objectivity, professed spirituality becomes an affront and an obstacle to the very spirit of truth that it professes to seek.

Chapter 8

The Reality of Santa Claus

The unfortunate reality about Santa Claus, that most of us eventually come to terms with in life, is that he doesn't exist as represented. By some accounts, there was once a character whose life contributed to the exaggerated myth that we now pass on from generation to generation. Be that as it may, the reality is that Santa Claus, as currently and traditionally represented to our hopeful children year after year as Christmas day approaches, is a gross mythical fabrication and an interesting and revealing commentary on our culture and on our-selves. Most Christians lie to their children to perpetuate the good feelings and good values associated with a myth. We find ourselves under considerable social pressure to perpetuate this lie. Most of us don't feel apologetic or uncomfortable in doing so. The end, we think, justifies the means. Perhaps it does. Perhaps it doesn't. I will leave that to you, the reader, to decide for yourself. Meanwhile, I'd like you to consider with me some of the philosophical ramifications of this annual social exercise that Christians call Christmas.

Are we bad people for perpetuating this lie for our children's sake? Are we mistaken in thinking that the good that might come of it outweighs the loss of credibility and questions that it gives rise to in later life? Should this narrow aspect of our lives be deemed a sufficient basis for assessing our overall "badness" or "goodness", or should a broader range of behavior be factored in? If, on the basis of a broader range of behavior, we qualify for being seen as good people, does that "goodness" make the myth of Santa Claus true because good people perpetuate the myth? Are we not sincere? Does our sincerity make the myth of Santa Claus true? Should our testimonies in other matters be seen with doubt, since we lied about this thing? Are people who come to doubt the myth of Santa Clause bad for doubting it? Am I over-thinking the matter? Are these questions contentious and evil? Is there anything constructive that can come out of them?

Is it possible that Joseph Smith might have come to believe that he was doing a good thing by piecing together a belief system that made more sense to him than the prevailing ones at hand? Is it possible that Joseph Smith might have been a little more liberal with his definition of a "revelation" than some, and considered that what occurred to him was attributable to God if it made sense and seemed to have some measure of arguable historical and Biblical consistency? Do we not sometimes attribute inspiration to men whose contributions to the human family are notable, even though they make no pretense of any unique relationship with God? Would they be less inspired if they made a claim of Godly authority that couldn't be authenticated in other ways? What if they were sinners while at the same time great contributors to human progress and social justice? What if they were hypocrites? Should they be stripped of their credit for inspiration under such circumstances? How can one answer such questions? Is it really necessary to answer such questions? What is truth? What is the value of truth? What is the relevance of truth to our lives?

I have come to believe that inner peace is found in accepting truth to be the reality of the universe as it actually is, apart from our social and emotional biases. I believe inner peace is best pursued by accepting the challenge of reconciling our lives to the realities of the universe to the best of our ability with integrity and authenticity as much as possible, no matter what anyone else thinks or wants us to do or be. I have come to accept that truth is the reality of things as they are, apart from me and my perceptions of them. Truth is. It is not what I want it to be or wish it to be. It just is. I may perceive it accurately. I may not. My challenge is to strive to improve my perceptive powers to see the realities of the universe around me for what they actually are, no matter what I or anyone else wants, or emotionally or socially needs them to be. Perhaps the most meaningful step, in developing sufficient self-awareness to embark on a lifelong quest to apprehend truth for what it actually is, will be to come to understand and accept our own fallibilities and human weaknesses, particularly as they relate to our perceptions. We must understand that we are emotional beings as much as intelligent beings and that our emotions impact on our perceptions. We must come to be aware of and accept that our emotions do not necessarily enhance the accuracy of our perceptions, but rather, more often than not, warp them. As this is the case, and it most certainly is the case, in my experience, we must, if we really want to understand reality for what it actually is, develop methods and techniques for seeing reality past our emotions and social pressures, without allowing them to warp our perceptions due to fear, desire, pride, shame or politics. The transient pain of learning that reality may not be what we once thought it was, or felt that we needed it to be, or wanted it to be, is, for me, well worth the inner peace and quiet confidence of understanding that harmony with the actuality of reality is the only rational and sustainable course for man. I believe it is the course that has the greatest hope and chance of maximizing whatever happiness and peace may be found in life. Harmony is integrity. Harmony is respect for the universe, as it is. It is respect for our fellow man, in his journey, and rights, apart from our own. It requires of us restraint, self-control, self-awareness, and legitimate volitional action, not necessarily to satisfy the arbitrary demands of a professed priesthood, or self limiting cultures, but to satisfy the actual demands of an unforgiving universe and the realities of the cosmos on all levels, as we reconcile our lives with the realities of that universe. With or without a Supreme Being as its Creator, the universe around us exists in reality and requires of us behavior that is consistent with and respectful of that reality and all of its ramifications to survive and to prosper. It is our right to survive and prosper in harmony. It is an inalienable right of all of mankind to pursue survival and prosperity in an environment free of coercion, oppression, or manipulative deception. We each have this right and we each owe this right to our fellow man with or without a belief in God. Respect for this right is fundamental to social justice. Social justice is unsustainable without broad respect for this right. Social justice is vital to the survival and prosperity of our species. Social justice is harmony.

Let us imagine, for conversation's sake, that there is a God. Let us imagine, for the purposes of this discussion, that He is the God as defined by the Mormon theology. He, among other things, then, is both just and unchanging. The universe, as we have come to understand it, is unforgiving in its requirements that we live in accordance with its laws. We cannot defy those laws. We must harmonize our lives with those laws to survive and prosper. According to the Mormon theology, those laws are His laws. Justice is integral to those laws, and to His character, and to His requirements of us as human beings. The "work and the glory" of the Mormon God is to "bring to pass the immortality and eternal life of man", (*Pearl of Great Price, Selections from the Book of Moses.* See page 4 of the 1981 edition.) within the context of freedom of choice. Eternal life is characterized by omniscience, among other things, which is the ultimate manifestation of intelligence. Freedom of choice allows men to choose between eternal damnation and eternal life. According to the Mormon theology, God has appointed a priesthood to represent Him in an environment that strictly prohibits coercion, or manipulation, or dishonesty as a method of conversion. Integrity and honesty are absolute conditions of exaltation, but are only credited to those who exhibit such by making a choice in an environment of freedom to exercise a different choice. Were this not so, intelligence would be openly undermined. The Mormon *Doctrine and Covenants* specifically provides:

> Behold, there are many called, but few are chosen. And why are they not chosen? Because their hearts are so set on the honors of men, that they do not learn this one lesson -- That the rights of the priesthood are inseparably connected with the powers of heaven, and that the powers of heaven cannot be controlled nor handled only upon the principles of righteousness. That they may be conferred upon us, it is true; but when we undertake to cover our sins, or to gratify our pride, our vain ambition, or to exercise control or dominion or compulsion upon the souls of the children of men, in any degree of unrighteousness, behold, the heavens withdraw themselves; the Spirit of the Lord is grieved; and when it is withdrawn, Amen to the priesthood or the authority of that man. (*Doctrine & Covenants, Section 121.* Compare to page 242 of the 1981 edition.)

Similarly, the *Doctrine and Covenants* records the Lord's declaration, "that every man may act in doctrine and principle ... according to the moral agency which I have given unto him, that every man may be accountable for his own sins in the day of judgment." (*Doctrine & Covenants, Section 101.* See page 199 of the 1981 edition)

It makes sense that men who make good choices shouldn't be credited with inherent goodness, if the alternative bad choices have been made unavailable to them. Similarly, it is unfair that men are condemned as inherently bad for making bad choices, when no good choices are available to them. Neither would be justice, but rather foolishness on the part of the judge. We would like to think that God is not a fool. Unfortunately, the doctrines of some and the practices of others who attribute their practices to Him, make Him out to be a fool by implication.

There may be some controversy about the accuracy of the details of historical accounts a Mormon Bishop, under the ecclesiastical "jurisdiction" of Brigham Young, castrating a young man who would not yield to their authority and, in one particular account, the specific application of that authority being a demand that the young man willingly give up his fiancé to become a polygamist wife to the Bishop, but there should be no question about the inconsistency of this type of priesthood authority with the published and canonized doctrinal constraints that apply to that authority in the Mormon theology. Accordingly, assuming, for the sake of conversation of the principles involved, that this account is true, the behavior of the Bishop is not necessarily an indictment of the authority of the Church, but rather evidence of the Bishop's own personal corruption, and insanity, and a basis for his removal from the priesthood. If, however, Brigham Young subsequently upheld the priesthood authority of such a Bishop, as Church apologists seem to agree that he did, the legitimacy of the authority of Brigham Young could, and should, be called into question on the basis of its overt inconsistency with the doctrine of the Church on the subject of that authority. I submit to the reader that the true character of a man or an organization is not so much revealed in individual departures from acceptable standards, but rather how the individuals and institutions in question respond to being confronted with the reality that such departures have occurred. Truth is legitimately supported by truth and consistency. Legitimate authority cannot defy its own limitations. Immediately, when it does, it distinguishes itself as corrupt and unworthy of loyalty or obedience and should never again be seen to be legitimate as long as it attempts to maintain its legitimacy in defiance of the very principles of its existence. This principal was recognized by the founding fathers of the United States of

America, who, in their Declaration of Independence acknowledged,

> When in the Course of human events, it becomes neces-
> sary for one people to dissolve the political bands which
> have connected them with another, and to assume among
> the powers of the earth, the separate and equal station to
> which the Laws of Nature and of Nature's God entitle
> them, a decent respect to the opinions of mankind requires
> that they should declare the causes which impel them to
> the separation. We hold these truths to be self-evident, that
> all men are created equal, that they are endowed by their
> Creator with certain unalienable Rights, that among these
> are Life, Liberty and the pursuit of Happiness. That to
> secure these rights, Governments are instituted among
> Men, deriving their just Powers from the consent of the
> governed, — That whenever any Form of Government
> becomes destructive of these ends, it is the Right of the
> People to alter or to abolish it, and to institute new Gov-
> ernment, laying its foundation on such principles and or-
> ganizing its powers in such form, as to them shall seem
> most likely to effect their Safety and Happiness. (*Declara-
> tion of Independence*)

Liberty is fundamental and key to the rights of American citizens and the legitimacy of the authority that they have vested in their political leaders. Freedom of choice, referred to in the Mormon theology as "free agency", is fundamental and key to the legitimate authority of God's priesthood.

Neither coercion nor deception is permitted in the maintenance of the priesthood of God in the Mormon theology. The very use of such tactics invalidates the priesthood authority itself. It follows necessarily, that the advocacy or support of continued priesthood authority in defiance of these principles would be self-defeating for its inconsistency with the governing principles that apply. Accordingly, to be consistent with the demands of the Mormon priesthood, as defined in the Mormon doctrine, integrity must be maintained in the priesthood. This is not to say that there won't be departures, fallible men being who and what they are. However, if God is just and not a fool about the fallibility of men, then it would seem that He must require of His authorized agents that a meaningful system of redress and discipline be in place which never permits the continued use of priesthood authority by one who will not uphold the principles upon which it is based. Neither, if God is just, should any who refuse to support the principles upon which the priesthood is based, and submit themselves to the same standards of repentance, by acknowledgement and restitution, that are imposed on the members, be allowed to enter the temple of God or serve in the priesthood. It would seem reasonable that the same worthiness standards imposed upon the lay members should apply to their leaders. To deny the strict application of these standards is, by Mormon doctrine itself, tantamount to a denial of the legitimacy of the priesthood authority of God itself. For me, the notion that Brigham Young, God's leading representative on earth at the time, would cavalierly look past a castration of a member to exact compliance and terrorize other members into submission, by upholding the priesthood authority of such a Bishop, should be recognized as considerable evidence in support of the conclusion that the Church's claim to legitimate authority is false. The fact of the actual castration is not the larger philosophical issue, as it relates to the legitimacy of the authority of the Church. If the Bishop was appropriately dealt with, the question of the legitimacy of authority in the Church could be isolated to the Bishop, himself. Otherwise, the Church, itself, becomes an accomplice to the questionable behavior by tacit approval. The fact that most devout Mormons can't or won't follow this reasoning speaks volumes about the impact on their reasoning faculties and sense of ethics that the "Gift of the Holy Ghost" has, and which is supposed to enlighten them beyond the level of their non-Mormon counterparts due to their worthiness. God help the man who is tried before a jury made of up enlightened Mormons with the "gift of the Holy Ghost" who "feel" he is a threat to their faith and priesthood authority.

Somewhere along the line we confirm to our children that their growing suspicions that there is no Santa Claus are correct. Ultimately, we decide that the game has served its purpose in their childhood, and, as they get older, we see that grasping truth for what it actually is and not being seen to be a fool among their peers is a higher value. I wonder what would happen if no one ever told them there was no Santa Claus, and they were subjected throughout their lives to enormous social pressure including being ostracized for openly doubting. Should they be condemned as fools under such circumstances? More significantly, is there any real moral, intellectual, or faith-based benefit to the continuation of their belief under such circumstances?

I submit to you that the young child who observed that the emperor had no clothes, in Hans Christian Andersen's famous tale, did not exhibit keener insight than his parents, that came as a result of years of study and practice with observations. No, this was not the case, nor was it the point of the story. What he observed was plain to see and required no special powers of perception, but only the absence of the corruption of those powers of perception by social forces and political biases. The fable itself was actually a political commentary of the day, told as a fable to avoid condemnation and punishment brought upon the author for openly observing and commenting on the obvious impotence of the current leadership and the circular condemnation that dissenters could expect to come upon them. Two weavers in the story promise the emperor a suit of new clothes that is invisible to people who are unqualified for their positions, or, otherwise, incompetent. Not wanting to be brought under such condemnation, no one is willing to acknowledge that the emperor has no clothes on when he dawns his new suit.

The weavers exploit the opportunity created by everyone's social dependency and fear of condemnation by creating a suit of clothes that doesn't exist. They accomplished broad public acquiescence to a ridiculous falsehood by employing the coercive tool of social condemnation. It took a young boy with nothing socially at risk to recognize and comment on what no one else dared. Dissention is a risky thing. If I had not already asked to have my name removed from the records of the Mormon Church, I would most certainly be excommunicated on the basis of this publication. My family will find it necessary to help the younger children among them understand that I am corrupt and not worthy of listening to, and otherwise protect them from extended exposure to me in order to preserve their delicate testimonies. It has already been suggested that visits with some of my grandchildren should be supervised so that my evil influence can be monitored and an adult can step in, when necessary, and bring the meeting to a conclusion. There will be a need to exaggerate and promote rumors of my failings in life, attributing them to my rotten character, and accentuate every professed challenge to my credibility. Considerable evidence that this has been ongoing for years has been witnessed, not only by me, but by others who have been kind enough to report their observations to me. The last thing my family will find time for is a fair hearing of things I've been accused of. The presumption of my guilt serves intense social and emotional purposes.

Ironically, I still believe in Santa Claus. I just understand him differently. Even more ironically, I still believe that Joseph Smith was a prophet. I just understand the meaning of the term "prophet" differently. For instance, I now understand that a prophet can also be a fraud, a con, a psychotic, and a sexual deviant. They are not mutually exclusive concepts. Neither is the concept of prophecy necessarily synonymous with legitimate authority from God. These are important distinctions. They are not distinctions given a great deal of attention in the Mormon theology. They are not distinctions that will ingratiate me to my Mormon family. They are, however, distinctions that help me see the universe for what it actually is as opposed to what I once wished it might be. Joseph Smith exhibited uncommon insight and anticipated some things correctly. Among other things, he anticipated, with uncommon accuracy, the naiveté of men and the lengths they would go to pursue their desires to believe and, more significantly, their social desires to belong. He anticipated, with historically profound insight, the degree to which such sincere desires could be exploited. He anticipated the astounding degree with which intelligent human beings would employ a self-imposed filter of selective blindness to maintain their social alliances. There is no question in my mind that Joseph Smith was a prophet. I don't think the occasional castration of dissenters was even necessary. I would be surprised to learn that Joseph Smith or Brigham Young ever encouraged it. It makes no difference to me, however, because I think that tacitly condoning abuse of authority by arguing in favor of, or otherwise, defending the continuing support of the priesthood authority of those who commit such acts is noteworthy and inescapable in its expository value for the question of the legitimacy of the claim of authority from a just God.

Chapter 9

The Emergence of Doubt

As I contemplate the historical emergence of my own doubts about the authenticity of the claims of the Mormon Church, I realize that there is something quite curious, while at the same time oddly understandable, about my journey. As it turns out, what caught my attention and shook me out of a state of willful blindness to very real and very relevant questions were fairly simple injustices and inequities in priesthood behavior that I think most Mormons would not even consider very noteworthy. They involved unfairness to others, not to me, and sometimes simple absurdities where positions taken by priesthood leaders were irreconcilable with Church doctrine but upheld for what seemed to be local political reasons. I began to question the integrity of the priesthood on the basis of my experience with it as a Counselor in two successive Bishoprics. I did not witness any castrations or other such atrocities. I just saw simple inequities and absurdities that I could not reconcile with an intelligent God and which gave rise to the first level of obvious questions. Then, what really struck me profoundly, was seeing unacceptable and indefensible behavior by lower priesthood authorities supported and tacitly endorsed by an unwillingness of higher authorities to hold the lower authorities accountable to the Church's own doctrinal standards. This was the big "tipoff" for me. Members are routinely counseled to overlook the inappropriate behavior of their priesthood leaders in the spirit of forgiveness and faith in God. This counsel takes on the form of pressure when worthiness is questioned for not letting things go that the priesthood authorities would rather not deal with. The real curiosity that I now see is that all through the years I had completely overlooked something that I, myself, had intimate personal knowledge of, and that I now recognize to be among the more powerful evidences of doctrinal inconsistencies and inappropriate use of priesthood authority that I had personally witnessed. For decades I didn't even give it much thought, while being taken with other more insignificant things. I now realize the extent to which I, personally, participated in the willful blindness that is so typical of cultish devotion. Interestingly, I asked to have my name removed from the records of the Church, having concluded that I could not support the claims of the Church's divine authority on the basis of experiences that I considered to be sufficiently conclusive to compel my withdrawal long before it ever occurred to me that something, which I had, myself, overlooked for decades, was completely and glaringly inappropriate and inconsistent with the professed doctrine of the Church.

While a young member of the Mormon Melchizedek priesthood, I heard a very significant and noteworthy confession. More noteworthy than the confession, was how the situation was handled by the Church. It would be an inappropriate violation of privacies and priesthood confidentiality for me to disclose the name of the individual involved. I will, however, take license from the example of countless General Authorities of the Church, who so often tell of confessions from the pulpit in their addresses at Church conference time, to illustrate various faith-promoting points to the members of the Church. In this particular case I am reconciled that disclosure of the substance of the confession, without identifying the individual involved, is warranted because of the gravity of what is illustrated by what followed as it relates to the claims of the Church of Jesus Christ of Latter Day Saints about its own divine authority from God. The confession involved the

commission of a very serious sexual crime. The circumstances under which I heard the confession were "privileged"
and so my report of the confession would not be admissible
as evidence in a court of law.

A young, recently married, woman came to her Bishop with
her new husband to discuss a matter that she had recently
disclosed to the husband. She had served a mission for the
Church, and was regular in her attendance at the Mormon
temple, and had been recently married in the temple, all on
the basis of her professed worthiness, and the satisfaction of
numerous priesthood officials, who had interviewed her with
respect to her worthiness, that she was telling the truth. This
priesthood satisfaction, as to her worthiness, was based on
the professed spiritual feelings of confirmation to priesthood
officials that she was worthy. Now she stunned the Bishop,
who she had known for years, with the confession that prior
to her missionary service for the Mormon Church, as a
young woman, she had repeatedly molested a baby boy that
was entrusted to her care as a baby sitter. She had become
obsessed with masturbation and gravitated from simple self-
manipulation, to self-manipulation with external objects,
and, ultimately, used a naked baby boy entrusted to her care
as a baby sitter to facilitate her orgasms. She had been
wracked with guilt for years. She was now moved by her
husband's love, and acceptance, and personal devotion to
purging from himself, by repentance and confession,
everything he felt he needed to purge from his own soul. She
decided she needed to get this cleared up by confessing it to
her husband and Church officials, as is consistent with the
doctrine of the Mormon Church on the subject of repentance
from serious offenses. She also confessed to various other
sexual encounters in her earlier life, which, by Mormon
standards, should have been confessed to Church authorities
prior to her missionary service. It was now clear that she had
lied countless times, throughout the previous years, having
been a party to regular and routine interviews with

priesthood officials in which she was asked if there was anything in her life that had not been confessed, which should have been confessed previously, as a condition of worthiness to enter the temple and serve the Church as an official representative in missionary service. She had also lied to her husband, misrepresenting to him that she was worthy for a temple marriage by Mormon standards.

To fully appreciate the significance of this scenario, one needs to understand the Mormon doctrine on the subject of repentance and worthiness. Mormons believe that the maintenance of an individual's worthiness, for temple attendance and exaltation in the next life, requires repentance from sin. The process of repentance, for Mormons, involves certain doctrinal requirements. Missionaries who serve the Church in the "mission field" are taught this process in specific detail. Considerable Mormon literature is dedicated to the process, including the *Miracle of Forgiveness,* by Spencer Kimball, a former president of the Church of Jesus Christ of Latter Day Saints and who, incidentally, spoke briefly at my grandmother Vilate Lee Romney's funeral in Salt Lake City many years ago, together with his first councilor in the first presidency of the Mormon Church at the time, Marion G. Romney.

For Mormons, the process of repentance requires the following steps: First, confession of the sin to one's self, to God in prayer, to the offended party or parties where another individual or individuals are involved, and for sins of a particularly serious nature, to an appropriate authority of the Church, most typically one's Bishop. Clearly, child molestation and all other forms of sexual transgression, including fornication and adultery, would require confession to a Church authority, by Mormon standards. Moving on, one must ask for forgiveness and offer restitution, wherever possible, and demonstrate willingness to make things right, in an appropriate way, with the offended party or parties.

This process of restitution should not be limited to a perfunctory declaration of willingness. It requires actual follow-through. Accordingly, theft, for instance, would require restitution satisfactory to the victim for the process of repentance to be considered complete.

In the Mormon theology, sexual sin is an "abomination" and is considered among the most serious of sins, in some cases approximating murder. In a noteworthy scripture from the *Book of Mormon*, very familiar to most members, the prophet, Alma, explains to his son that sexual sins are "an abomination in the sight of the Lord; yea, most abominable above all sins save it be the shedding of innocent blood or denying the Holy Ghost". (*Book of Mormon, The Book of Alma.* Compare to page 306 of the 1981 edition.) For this reason, sexual related transgressions, for members, often involve the convening of "Church disciplinary courts" in which Church authorities may determine that the repentance process for the behavior in question may require a period of "probation", or that the member should be "disfellow-shipped", or "excommunicated". Less noteworthy sins are handled, at the discretion of the Bishop, without convening "Church courts", and with more informal counseling and prescribed steps of repentance, often involving abstaining from weekly sacrament for a contemplative period of time during which follow-up interviews with the Bishop are scheduled to monitor the member's spiritual progress with the required change of heart appropriate to the infraction. With this in mind, I will leave it to the reader to consider where, on this sliding Mormon scale of seriousness, the repeated rape of a baby boy might fall.

The Mormon Bishops are specifically and uniquely "called" to be "judges in Israel" for the purpose of assessing these situations brought before them and seeing to it that the standards of the Church are maintained and the worthiness of the members is lovingly encouraged by requiring of the member, as a condition of temple worthiness, the prescribed course of repentance. Bishops have some limited measure of discretionary leeway in the application of Church standards, but consult heavily with their regional "Stake Presidencies" and the general *Church Handbook of Instructions* issued to all Bishops by the Church.

Now most of us have sufficient knowledge and experience in our communities, and exposure to the local and national news, to have come to realize that it is naive to expect absolute consistency in the application of the prosecutorial discretion of local district attorneys. We know that budget constraints, politics, sometimes corruption, and career related motivations can impact on local prosecutor's choices of what to invest time in "bringing to justice" and what to overlook. Believers in God, and in a uniquely authorized priesthood agency to administer God's justice to His children on earth in a way that is actually just and unchanging, would like to believe that more consistency is reasonable to expect of God's priesthood agents. Mormon's are particularly reminded that when the use of God's priesthood is applied to "...cover our sins, or to gratify our pride, our vain ambition, or to exercise control or dominion or compulsion upon the souls of the children of men, in any degree of unrighteousness, behold, the heavens withdraw themselves; the Spirit of the Lord is grieved; and when it is withdrawn, Amen to the priesthood or the authority of that man." (*Doctrine & Covenants, Section 121*. Compare to page 242 of the 1981 edition.) Accordingly, inexplicable inconsistencies in the application of God's justice, especially where those inconsistencies might conveniently spare the Church itself or individual priesthood members some measure of embarrassment, would be, understandably, quite unseemly.

In this particular scenario, the Bishop, having heard the disturbing confession of the wife, called the husband into his office to join them. He then advised the husband that he was entitled to an annulment of their recent temple marriage on the basis of the wife's deception in misleading both himself and the Church as to her worthiness for the temple marriage. The annulment, however, would be a choice that the husband would have to make, after considering the alternative choice of forgiveness. The Bishop asked the husband to pray about his decision and meet again with the Bishop in a few days to advise the Bishop of his prayerful decision. Obviously, forgiveness was encouraged. The young man was a recently returned Mormon missionary, having preached repentance and forgiveness to newly converted members for the past two years. Upon return from his mission, and under considerable cultural pressure from the Church, which was typical at that time, he felt it was his next priority and duty in life to marry. He fell in love with his wife. She too, was a recent missionary. They were married in the temple after a brief courtship and had returned from their honeymoon very recently. Bereft and confused, but wanting to be forgiving, this young, inexperienced, and naive man told his wife and the Bishop that he wanted to stay married and love his wife through the process of repentance. On this basis, amazingly, the young woman was simply told to quietly refrain from taking the sacrament and attending the temple for a short period of time, and to make her confessions in writing to other Church officials she had involved in the deception, including her former mission president. She did so. Her former mission president was a General Authority of the Church at the time. He responded to her letter with loving and forgiving tones, forgave her for her offense of lying to him and told her that the Lord would forgive her and, interestingly, that she should never speak of this matter again. Likewise, another General Authority of the Church quietly forgave, but required nothing significant of her in the repentance process. There was no Church "disciplinary court" and no requirement of confession or restitution to the offended parties to complete the process of repentance. After a brief period, her temple privileges were reinstated and she has continued to enjoy full fellowship in the Church ever since, even serving in significant Church callings requiring exemplary standards of worthiness. She has never confessed the matter to the offended parties.

Individuals in the very same ecclesiastical region of the Church, having committed lesser offenses, have been excommunicated from the Church on the basis of those offenses. In the case of this woman, priesthood officials up and down the entire ecclesiastical rank and file of the priesthood from the local Bishop to the President of the Church, himself, had approved of her missionary call on the basis of their priesthood powers of inspiration, confirming God's call to her on the basis of her worthiness. An un-convicted child molester had represented the Church of Jesus Christ of Latter Day Saints in missionary service for eighteen months, all the while enjoying the sustaining support of her priesthood leaders, on the basis of their ongoing findings of worthiness, all based on professed spiritual insight after repeated interviews prior to and throughout her mission. She deceived them all, their exclusive agency and unique priesthood powers of revelation relevant to their jurisdiction notwithstanding. She was now rewarded for her deceit with a relative slap on the wrist in what seems to me to be an alarming inconsistency of Church discipline. The inconsistency seems to be inexplicable in any way, other than to save the Church public embarrassment and the awkward position of finding themselves in the position of having to excuse their culpability for the inappropriate approvals of her service by denying the effectiveness of their own powers of inspiration, as it related to her calling to missionary service.

I am personally aware that what I have described above actually occurred. I heard the verbal confessions with my own ears. I saw the written confessions with my own eyes and handled the correspondence with my own hands, including the letters of reply from two General Authorities of the Church. I was a young, naive member of the Mormon priesthood at the time, and I am ashamed to admit that I did not recognize the inappropriateness of the situation until after I had already asked to have my name removed from the records of the Church for other reasons, also involving the ethics of the priesthood on less severe levels over two decades later. I am sure there will be those who, on the basis of my apostasy from the Mormon Church, will surmise that I am fabricating, exaggerating, or somehow misrepresenting this story. There will be members of the Church, even perhaps members of the priesthood, who will take advantage of the cultural and social biases against me as an apostate, among members of the Church, by encouraging the belief that I am not telling the truth and am motivated by a dark and evil spirit in making a point of these matters. I have already been subjected to years of this type of spin at the hands of Mormons who have a deep social interest in the belief that I am evil. I have been lied to by temple recommend holding Mormons, lied about by temple recommend holding Mormons, cheated in business by temple recommend holding Mormons, and falsely accused, set up, framed, and personally threatened by those who know of my apostasy. Some of these people are members of my own family. I surmise that they justify their behavior towards me on the basis of my apostasy. I now live largely in seclusion. I have decided to publish my account because I don't know how much longer I will have the opportunity to do so and I think I owe it to those to whom I previously shared my testimony of the "truthfulness of the Church". I was sincere then. I am sincere now in saying that I was wrong then. That is not to say that I am a perfect man. I, myself, have engaged in behavior that I am not proud of. I have also engaged in behavior that Mormons would condemn, but that I no longer have a problem with. Every day I strive to make my peace with God, the universe, and my fellow man. I strive for harmony and am aware that I still fall short of it. I no longer strive to "conform" my life and choices to the arbitrary will of an external priesthood that professes unique authority from God and the right to dictate conditions of my worthiness on that basis. I believe that goodness of the soul can be achieved without the permission or the direction of the Mormon priesthood. I believe that true goodness of the soul is <u>better</u> achieved without the permission and direction of the Mormon priesthood.

The handling of the situation of the former child molester by the Mormon priesthood bears consideration. I would like to share some observations in that regard. Mormon repentance requires confession. Mormon worthiness requires repentance. The Mormon God is both just and unchanging. The Mormon priesthood authority requires integrity in the ministry and expressly prohibits the misapplication of priesthood authority for the purpose of "covering the sins" of the priesthood itself. In the case of the child molester, the Mormon priesthood found itself with a conflict of interest in administering the justice of God. The reality of the temple marriage and prior missionary service of the child molester is de-facto evidence of a consistent pattern of the absence of the very unique spiritual enlightenment ("revelation") that the Mormon priesthood professes to possess and use on behalf of God in calling God's servants to positions of responsibility in the ministry. Open and noteworthy news of this situation would have placed the Church in a very awkward publicity position. The confession of the child molester to the offended parties would have very likely resulted in broad public exposure of the situation and the incarceration of the woman on the basis of her own confession. The woman would have had a clear motivation to avoid confession to the offended parties. This motivation was consistent with the Church's motivation, but inconsistent with the Church's doctrine of repentance. Also, the Church's priesthood is, by its own parameters, prohibited from "compulsion" in applying its principles. The Church, even if it chose to recommend confession to the woman, could not "compel" her to confess to the offended parties. It could, however, deny a temple recommend to the woman until such time as she reported that she had confessed of her own free will and choice. I believe this would have been consistent with the Church's own applicable and published doctrines on the subject. Unfortunately, the risk that the woman would forever after feel unworthy, for lack of admission to the Mormon temple, until she confessed to the offended parties, might have motivated her to do so. This would have been an embarrassment to the Church. The Church's handling of the matter was consistent with the Church's publicity interests, but inconsistent with its own published doctrinal positions on the subject. In fairness to the Bishop involved, I recognize that he was a kindly man who must have experienced a significant struggle with this situation. What good could possibly have come to the family whose trust had been violated by a confession at this point? It would have been easy for the Bishop to surmise that no lasting harm had come of the matter, since the infant would probably have no recollection of the event and the parents didn't know. Would alerting them now make anyone's life better? The former molester had dedicated herself to devoted Church service for years in an effort to purge her soul of her offenses and demonstrated a completely contrite and remorseful anxiety about the situation. Shouldn't she be permitted and encouraged to get on with her life in peace? What good could possibly come of her public humiliation at this point? I understand and appreciate the dilemma of the Bishop. I have no problem with the husband's forgiveness for the woman or forgiveness for her in general. I am troubled, however, by the Church's self serving inconsistency in the handling of the matter. In my sincere opinion, the husband should not have been counseled to continue the marriage, but rather to accept the annulment as an appropriate remedy giving everyone involved a badly needed "time-out" to more thoughtfully consider the considerable

consequences and ramifications of the matter. The
trivialization of the matter by the Church did a great
disservice to the family involved. The handling of the matter
was not consistent with a reasonable application of the
published doctrines of the Church, nor was it consistent with
the best interests of the emerging family in question that
suffered for decades with the emotional scars of a haunted
woman, in desperate need of therapy, and a man, also
unequipped to take on the challenge of a family in his own
way. The marriage ultimately resulted in divorce and
significant emotional distress for the entire family including
the ongoing injustice of a pre-emptive and unfair campaign
to vilify the husband, in an effort to damage his credibility as
a hedge against the eventuality that he might disclose what
he knows and embarrass the wife and the Church.

There is no question that the marriage was based on false
pretenses that were relevant to the marital covenants and
mutual understandings of the parties. More significantly, the
woman required a "temple worthiness recommend" to be
married in the temple which she acquired as the result of a
fraudulent representation of worthiness by Mormon
standards. Accordingly, the marriage was a fraud. I believe
that a consistent God, as defined by the Mormons, would
have seen the annulment of the marriage not to have been at
the discretion of the husband, but rather, mandatory, on the
basis of the reality of the situation. Entitlement to a temple
marriage is not at the discretion of the husband, but the
discretion of God according to the doctrines that apply. The
doctrines were violated. The priesthood made an arbitrary
decision to waive the applicability of the doctrines in a set of
circumstances that served the publicity purposes of the
Church. In this way the Church contributed to considerable
distress and heartache in the lives of a future family, who
had no business embarking on a marriage under such
circumstances, while hiding its own shame. It was a difficult
decision for the Bishop. I understand that. He should not be

condemned, but neither should the Church be credited with "inspiration" in this thing. Rather, I think, a serious fallibility with the idea of the administration of individual "worthiness" by an arbitrary priesthood was demonstrated. There are those, I suspect, who do not profess any particularly unique authority or divine powers of insight, who would agree that this was obvious.

The Mormon priesthood authorities will argue that God has the right to alter his own doctrinal standards at any time He sees fit and that the priesthood of God has the unique authority and rights to the "revelations" about such real-time adjustments as they may apply fluidly to situations as they arise. This is a convenient doctrinal position, indeed, and has basis in the Church's own publication, the *Doctrine and Covenants*. Curiously, the *Church Handbook of Instructions*, at the time I was a High Priest, called upon Bishops to weigh in the public notoriety of a situation in deciding upon the discipline to apply. Apparently the Church's administration of the justice of God needed to consider offenses that were widely known or that involved the Church's publicity interests to warrant a different measure of discipline than those that were quietly confessed. Unfortunately, this application of God's justice, even where it may be argued that God has the right to fluidly adjust the applicability of His own doctrine, leaves the observer with legitimate questions about fairness and the unchanging nature of God. Where different members of the Church are subjected to different standards of worthiness, it is difficult for reasonable people to condemn the obvious questions. Thoughtful members find themselves confronted with the difficult challenge to their faith that consists of a conflict. Either the priesthood is misrepresenting the justice of God, or God seems to be unfair and inconsistent in the application of His justice through the priesthood. The traditional spiritual emollient, consistently applied to this situation by the Church, is to encourage the members to suspend judgment which is reserved to God by overlooking the obvious inconsistency and trusting in the priesthood leadership with the promise that anything that seems unseemly will be rectified in God's "own due time". Challenges to their faith, they are told, are part of God's test of their worthiness, and refraining from being seen to criticize the priesthood becomes the deciding factor in such situations. Unfortunately, this formula renders the Church an inherently corruptible organization due to a self-serving doctrinal escape from accountability to consistently applied standards. According to the Mormon doctrine, God has acknowledged that "many are called but few are chosen" due to the openly declared corruptibility of men in positions of authority, as stated in the *Doctrine and Covenants*. It seems unlikely then, that God would foster intelligence and integrity as an integral part of the eternal progress required for exaltation by overlooking the need for a tight system of holding his priesthood and members accountable to consistently applied standards to avoid the very corruptibility that He foresees. It is particularly noteworthy that many examples of stricter accountability in the world of non-Mormon leadership authorities, including corporate management and judicial oversight through the process of meaningful appeal, are easily found. The society of non-Mormons, often referred to by Mormons as "gentiles", are presumed to be spiritually inferior and less enlightened for lack of the "Gift of the Holy Ghost" and unique powers of priesthood authority. This gives rise to questions about the intelligence of the Mormon God and consequently the authenticity and legitimacy of the Mormon priesthood.

Chapter 10

Enough

Seemingly countless volumes of material are published on the subject of Mormon theology and culture by critics of the Mormon Church. The Church itself has published countless volumes of material explaining its own doctrines and promoting a belief in its own authority. A detailed, point by point, analysis of every doctrine and historically significant event in the Church's history is not necessary to properly assess the Church's claim of unique and exclusive authority from God. Just as the Mormon Church teaches its missionaries to narrow the focus of investigators of the faith down to the epistemological formulas of the *Book of Mormon*, I similarly agree that a comprehensive review of "all things Mormon" is not necessary where a few simple fundamental realities provide conclusive evidence that is relevant to the question at hand.

Ironically, I agree with the Mormon Church that the epistemology of the *Book of Mormon* is a key, for exactly the opposite reason that investigators' attention is called to it by the Church. There is no question whatsoever in my mind that the epistemology advocated by the *Book of Mormon* prophets, as discussed in Chapter 3, above, is unquestionably recognizable as an unsound approach to the validation of truth. It encourages the suspension of the reasoning process in favor of a self-induced spiritual manifestation brought on by unleashing a desire to believe, combined with disrespect for the legitimate, necessary, and, vital role of skepticism to the intelligent process of reasonable evaluation of what is purported to be true, in a world known to be filled with deceit and trickery. I cannot believe a just and intelligent God would proscribe such an approach to the most serious questions of life. This approach serves the interests of the deceivers. Truth never needs to be served, supported, or propped up by the disparagement of objective and reasonable analysis. Illegitimate claims of priesthood authority always need to be supported by the disparagement of legitimate scrutiny, by calling it heresy or evil contention. I did not have the intellectual sophistication or experience in my youth to recognize this obvious clue in the Mormon doctrine and literature that belies the claims of the Church.

In addition to the problematic advocacy of the *Book of Mormon* epistemology, the Mormon Church defines its own priesthood out of existence, as it is consistently applied, up and down the ranks of the ecclesiastical leadership, in a manner the defies the very constraints of that priesthood, by the Church's own definition. There is no question in my mind that the General Authorities of the Church of Jesus Christ of Latter Day Saints are aware of unacceptably inconsistent applications of priesthood authority and consistently fail to take reasonable steps to hold the priesthood accountable to the doctrine of the Church. I am personally aware that temple recommends remain in force which defy the published standards of worthiness of the Church with the knowledge of priesthood leadership. I am personally aware that priesthood officials of the Church continue to be supported in their callings, notwithstanding the knowledge of their superior priesthood officials of legitimate concerns and complaints about the administration of their priesthood responsibility, resulting in offenses against members that have given rise to legitimate expectations of acknowledgement and restitution from priesthood officials whose authority is supported by the Church in the absence of such acknowledgements and restitution.

On the basis of the foregoing knowledge that I have of the Church of Jesus Christ of Latter Day Saints, I cannot accept, or be a party to, its claim that it truly has unique and divine authority in the ministry, nor that it is even a reasonable claim to make in light of the glaring realities that I am personally aware of. I believe that the Church systematically exploits the sincerity of the naïve, by requiring members to contribute enormous time, money, and talent to the Church, at great personal sacrifice, as a condition of worthiness for exaltation in the Kingdom of God, while promoting a belief that it is evil to employ the intellectual faculties every human being has been endowed with, by God, to see falsehood to be what it is and not mistake it for truth. Amidst this philosophical corruption, the Church continues, year after year, to purchase its way into credibility, notoriety, and public respectability with the enormous resources gleaned from its membership. It works diligently to avoid accountability to its own professed standards by suppression of the truth about its own conduct and historical realities through intimidation of its members with the looming threat of isolation, damnation, and vilification.

It is significant and noteworthy that The Church of Jesus Christ of Latter Day Saints is very different from other Protestant religions in very significant respects. Most Protestant religions do not make a claim of unique and exclusive authority from God to perform essential ordinances for exaltation in the Kingdom of God. Generally, a Protestant Pastor, or Minister, finds himself to be a part of the ministry as a result of a process that begins with a personal feeling of affinity and passion for both the faith in Jesus Christ and the prospect of being a part of the ministry of that faith. That feeling is generally deemed to be the substance of their "calling" to the ministry. On the basis of that feeling, they dedicate themselves, more fully, to studying the teachings of Jesus Christ as found in the Bible and, generally, enroll in colleges that prepare them for the avocation of Christian ministry. They are, ultimately, ordained into the ministry of their respective Protestant faiths and embark on making a career of the ministry. This ministry consists largely of advocating the teachings and principles of the Bible, and their beneficial merits, to whomsoever may hear their message, and encouraging prospective Disciples of Christ to follow His teachings as their hearts direct by the Spirit. Generally, the majority of the Protestant clergy does not represent their own unique agency of God to be the only agency through which members of the "body of Christ" may find exaltation in the "hereafter". To the contrary, members are generally encouraged to follow their faith in the teachings of Jesus Christ and build their life around His teachings to the best of their ability, as moved upon by the Spirit of the Lord. There may be some relatively minor controversies between ministries, as to some doctrinal details and their consistency with the Bible, but, for the most part, Protestant religions do not make particular and specific claims as to their exclusive rights to administer the priesthood authority of God. Contributions to Protestant ministries are accepted gratefully from members who are taught that such supportive giving is consistent with the teaching of the Bible. They do not, as a general rule, represent that they have unique authority from God to accept such gifts in partial, yet mandatory, satisfaction of the demands of God for the reward of exaltation in the next life. The Mormon religion is unique in this way... very unique. The difference is profound. The Protestant minister proclaims in effect, "I believe in the divinity of Jesus Christ. I have devoted my life to leaning of Him, and would like to share what I have learned with you, and encourage you to follow Him, and enter into a covenant with Him by your own faith." The Mormon priesthood proclaims in effect, "We are the uniquely authorized agents of God on earth, to the exclusion of all others, and have been called to declare to the world that we, alone, have the sole rights and keys to interpret and communicate the word of God to all of humanity and administer the ordinances of God which are required for exaltation in the hereafter. To reject our unique authority and interpretations of God's word is to reject God, Himself, and results in damnation."

The Protestant claim is simply a statement of faith and the encouragement of faith. The Mormon claim is an absolute declaration of unique authority to require specific things of candidates for exaltation. The Protestant claims cannot be challenged as deceptive because they are simply claims of faith. The Mormon claims require an entirely different threshold to be properly evaluated. The Mormon Prophets and Apostles do not simply claim to believe in the teachings of Jesus and recommend them to others. They profess to know the mind of God by virtue of their unique relationship with Him to the exclusion of all others. The legal ramifications of this are, or should be, significant. If a true believer were to openly profess a belief in Jesus Christ, and encourage others to explore His teachings, and contribute financially to that cause, such a person would not be committing a fraud by doing so. If, on the other hand, I said I saw God, and God told me that all other Churches are false, and that He endowed me with unique authority to represent Him on earth, and told me to tell you that He requires ten percent of your income be given to me, exclusively, as a condition of exaltation in the next life, I have now committed fraud, because I know that this is not true. If I convince you to give me your money on that basis and it is later discovered that I knew that such claims were not true, you can recover those funds from me in a legal action because my specific representations of unique knowledge and authority were the basis of your contributions. Similarly, if I proclaimed that I "knew" that someone else saw God, when, in fact, I knew no such thing, that would be equally dishonest. Generally, Protestant religions do not cross this line. They know it would be a fraud. They do not believe that they have such unique authority as the Mormons claim to have. The

Mormons cavalierly cross this line and have been doing so since the inception of the religion.

In my missionary training a significant point was made of the relevance, to investigators of the Church, of a particular scenario involving Martin Harris. Martin Harris was one of the three original witnesses who professed, in writing, to see the golden plates from which the *Book of Mormon* was translated. He left the Church, but according to the Mormons, never withdrew his testimony as having seen the golden plates. This, we are supposed to believe, supports the truth of the existence of those golden plates, as testified by the three witnesses. The naive are led to make the leap of logic that if he, Martin Harris, left the Church and never actually saw the golden plates that he previously professed in writing that he had, he surely would have retracted that former testimony at the time he left the Church. What naive investigators are not encouraged to consider, is that if he retracted his testimony as to the existence of the golden plates, he would have been immediately subjected to countless lawsuits for fraud brought by those who made significant contributions to the Church on the basis of his previous testimony that he had. I now understand these things. I came to understand them some years ago. For that reason, I ceased to officiate in the priesthood of the Mormon Church long before I actually asked to have my name removed from the records because I no longer believed it was true. Had I continued to profess it to be true while not actually believing it to be true, I would have been a party to a fraud.

I do not believe that the Church is true, nor do I believe that it is reasonable to think that the level of sophistication in education and experience amongst the senior leadership of the Church is too lacking for such men to be aware of the glaring inconsistencies between their own doctrines and the actual administration of their priesthood authority in defiance

of those doctrines. Neither do I believe it to be reasonable for
them to be unaware of the meaningful distinction between
knowledge and belief and the significant ramifications
involved in testifying that they know things to be true that
they not only have no reasonable basis for believing to be
true, but, to the contrary, are actually the custodians of a
preponderance of credible evidence that contradicts or
otherwise disproves those things. Accordingly, while I can
readily accept that Protestant ministries may well be sincere
in their faith, I believe that the Mormon ministry is a fraud
whose only plausible defense is self-delusion. I believe the
evidence of that fraud can be conclusively demonstrated in a
manner that should be sufficiently clear to reasonable people
who have respect for the intellectual process of objective
evaluation and a reasonable assessment of relevant
information that is widely available. For me, the obvious
fraud of the Mormon Church is far beyond a reasonable
doubt and an amazing commentary on an otherwise
seemingly intelligent group of people and the sheer power of
cultural and social pressure to warp an otherwise healthy
perspective of reality. The fact that many decent, sincere,
successful, and seemingly kindhearted people are Mormons
does not make the claims of their Church true. The claims of
the Mormon Church cannot stand the test of reasonable
scrutiny of all that is relevant to those claims, and so the
doctrine and culture of the Church has been constructed and
managed to encourage the disparagement of objective and
thorough scrutiny as an evil that should be avoided by the
faithful and a basis of disqualification from temple
worthiness and, in extreme cases, even membership. As a
matter of Church protocol, a Mormon cannot even
sympathize with an apostate to be considered worthy of
temple attendance. This is one of the mandatory temple
worthiness questions in the interview. "Do you sympathize
with any apostates?" A Mormon individual who spent
considerable time with me for a while suddenly informed me
that she had been threatened to be brought before the local

Mormon High Council on charges of sympathizing with an apostate. We were not romantically involved, so there was no other reason to question our friendship. I was abruptly informed that I was no longer welcome as a guest in her home. She had employment in a county where her boss was a high ranking official in the local Mormon Church. I surmised that she felt her employment was at risk. So, it would appear that the Mormon God declares with openness the potential for corruptibility of His priesthood in the *Doctrine and Covenants*, but disqualifies a member for temple worship for merely sympathizing with someone who may have left the Church over that corruption. Enlightened corporations, not professing unique authority of revelation from God, now conduct routine exit interviews in an effort to benefit from the potential of information coming out of legitimate complaints from former staff members in order to maintain the integrity of their corporate culture. The Mormon Church automatically and summarily condemns those who depart the faith, especially where the ethics of the priesthood is cited as the basis of their departure, and condemns any who may sympathize with their complaints. Of this, I am personally aware. The exploration of the possibility of the legitimacy of those complaints seems to be out of the question. It seems striking that the Mormon God would lack the insight into how to deal with the corruptibility of His own priesthood while such insight is demonstrated by certain corporate executives, some of whom actually fornicate and drink alcoholic beverages while being intolerant of injustice and duplicity in their ranks. Apparently the "trial" of a Mormon's faith, so often predicted by many Church leaders and *Book of Mormon* prophets, is to believe in a just God in spite of the fact that he is routinely represented to be patently unjust.

I no longer believe that the Mormon Church is true. I cannot sell out intellectual integrity and honesty for social acceptance. As it turns out, I remain with faith that one day I might be considered a decent human being in spite of my failings in life, worthy of at least some small measure of kindness and consideration from my fellow man without being a Mormon. I have ceased to seek such comfort amongst Mormons. I have come to realize that Joseph Smith was right about something else. True religion will require the sacrifice of all that one has to pursue it. My religion, now, is the simple pursuit of truth and quest for integrity, notwithstanding my human weakness, wherever it may be found. That pursuit has cost me all that I ever loved. I still think it's worth the price. I not only would sacrifice all that I have for it, I already have sacrificed all that I had for it, including the respect of most of my family and friends. I have nothing left but hope and belief in the merits of simple goodness, human decency, and a quest for integrity for no other reason than to feel comfortable with who looks back at me in the mirror. I want to respect that guy's struggle whether anyone else does or not. Meanwhile, my family prays that I might escape the evil clutches of Satan who has darkened my soul as a result of my own iniquity.

I deeply appreciate the time that you have taken to consider my thoughts on this subject. If you have found what I have offered to be constructive, I would very much appreciate hearing from you, to that effect. Your feedback is meaningful to me. I'd like to work constructively with those who are interested on projects involving the promotion of social justice, reasoned public policy, and respect for the process and relevance of objective reasoning in general.

The initial purpose and point of this project was to right the wrongs that I have committed by testifying to others, in sincere error, that the Church of Jesus Christ of Latter Day Saints is "true". Please help me to that end, by recommending this book to anyone who may be investigating the Church.

If you recognize me to be someone who participated, or was in any way involved, in your conversion to the Church, and feel inclined to contact me, I will look forward to hearing from you. I am obliged to make a gift of this book to you.

If you are a fellow refugee from the Mormon Church, and feel that I have captured the essence of things you would like to say to your family or friends, or converts, I would be deeply honored if you recommended this book to them for that purpose.

This is my restitution.

Further Reading / Bibliography

The Book of Mormon
© 1981 by Intellectual Reserve, Inc.
ISBN 978-59297-503-7
The Church of Jesus Christ of Latter Day Saints
Salt Lake City, Utah, USA

The Doctrine and Covenants
© 1981 by Intellectual Reserve, Inc.
ISBN 978-59297-503-7
The Church of Jesus Christ of Latter Day Saints
Salt Lake City, Utah, USA

The Pearl of Great Price
© 1981 by Intellectual Reserve, Inc.
ISBN 978-59297-503-7
The Church of Jesus Christ of Latter Day Saints
Salt Lake City, Utah, USA

Lectures on Faith
© 2000 by Covenant Communications, Inc.
ISBN 1-57734-637-8
Covenant Communications, Inc.
American Fork, Utah, USA

Teachings of the Prophet Joseph Smith
© 1976 by Deseret Book Company
ISBN 0-87747-626-8
Deseret Book Company
Salt Lake City, UTAH, USA

Democracy in America – Alexis de Tocqueville
Edited and abridges by Richard D. Heffner
© 1956 by Richard D. Heffner
Library of Congress Catalog Card No. 56-7402
Penguin Books USA Inc. (Mentor)
New York, NY, USA

The Virtue of Selfishness – Ayn Rand
© 1964 by Ayn Rand
© 1964 by The Objectivist Newsletter, Inc.
ISBN 0-451-15699-4
NAL Penguin Inc.
New York, NY, USA